PRAISE FOR *THE C*

"Difficult trials can challenge our faith or make the skeptic wonder whether God exists. Louie Giglio rightly notes that when we surrender ourselves to God, it's never too late for him to break through, because 'our circumstances don't inhibit God from fulfilling his plans and purposes.' Louie is one of the most influential writers and speakers in our time, and he has a deep and contagious passion for people and the gospel. I know his words will inform, inspire, and encourage you."

—Ravi Zacharias
Author and Speaker

"Louie Giglio is not just our friend, he's a leader who has inspired us again and again. *The Comeback* is truly a gift, and you should read every word."

—Mark Burnett and Roma Downey
Executive Producers, *Ben-Hur*
United Artists Media Group

"An instant classic and game-changing book from my friend Louie Giglio. *The Comeback* should be required reading for every leader. This book is inspiring, timely, challenging, and has massive potential to restore hope, reimagine possibilities, and reignite the passion for pursuing Jesus and making a difference in our world."

—Brad Lomenick
Past President of Catalyst
Author of *The Catalyst Leader* and *H3 Leadership*

"In a social media age of glossy and too-often-superficial portrayals of the human experience, Louie Giglio provides a raw and transparent look at the all-too-real fear, anxiety, worry, pain, and unrest that all of us will experience at one time or another. Drawn from real stories, including his own, and truths found in Scripture, *The Comeback* will encourage and strengthen the faith of anyone who reads it."

—Mark DeMoss
Founder, DeMoss

"We all love the story of a comeback in someone else's life; the person who has headed the wrong direction but by the grace of God is forever changed for the good. But we have problems showing ourselves the same grace when we need a comeback. Instead, self-criticism reigns. The truth is we all have moments when we need to come back to the provision of our loving God. Louie does a tremendous job highlighting the power of God and our need for a comeback no matter how far we are from the plan of God. This is a read for all of us in need of encouragement and inspiration to live the life God has called us to. Read these pages and start your comeback!"

—Gregg Matte
Pastor, Houston's First Baptist Church
Author of *Unstoppable Gospel*

"In *The Comeback* my friend Louie Giglio encourages us to remember just how much God loves underdogs. No matter the painful circumstances or depths of your loss, this book will speak to you with a wellspring of real hope. This book is an instant classic!"

—Chris Hodges
Senior Pastor, Church of the Highlands
Author of *Fresh Air* and *Four Cups*

"This is a book about hope and the invitation God gives us to rise above every obstacle. But it is not a book about the power of positive thinking. It is about the power that produces positive thinking—Jesus' victory over sin and death, which gives forgiveness for every sin, healing for every hurt, and life through every grace. These pages, like all of Louie's messages, will move you to reflect, teach you to believe, and inspire you to worship."

—J. D. Greer, PhD
Pastor of The Summit Church, Raleigh-Durham, North Carolina
Author of *Gaining by Losing*

"Louie personally knows what it takes to really believe it's never too late for God to restore forgotten dreams, lost relationships, unhealed wounds, and impossible circumstances. Honestly, this is a book we all need to read! You'll be empowered to take the first steps of your fresh start and achieve your ultimate comeback with God now."

—Lysa TerKeurst
New York Times Bestselling Author
President of Proverbs 31 Ministries

"Any discussion of a Comeback catches my attention. Any teaching by Louie Giglio touches my heart. To see the word *Comeback* on the cover of a book by Louie Giglio is a wonderful combination. This book will encourage all of us who daily depend on God's grace and mercy."

—Max Lucado
Pastor and Bestselling Author of *Glory Days*

THE COMEBACK

THE COMEBACK

IT'S NOT TOO LATE AND YOU'RE NEVER TOO FAR

LOUIE GIGLIO

W PUBLISHING GROUP

AN IMPRINT OF THOMAS NELSON

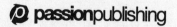

Published in Nashville, Tennessee, by W Publishing Group, an imprint of Thomas Nelson. W Publishing Group and Thomas Nelson are registered trademarks of HarperCollins Christian Publishing, Inc.

Thomas Nelson, Inc., titles may be purchased in bulk for educational, business, fund-raising, or sales promotional use. For information, please e-mail SpecialMarkets@ThomasNelson.com.

Library of Congress Control Number: 2015908317

ISBN 978-0-7180-4218-9 (HC)
ISBN 978-0-7180-7751-8 (ITPE)

Printed in the United States of America
16 17 18 19 RRD 12 11 10 9 8

CONTENTS

OVERTURE

THE STORMS, THE RAIN, AND THE WIND

We all share one thing in common. In all our lives there will be winds that blow. Headwinds of difficulty brought on by our own decisions and gale-force winds of adversity due to circumstances we never saw coming.

Yet, ultimately, God is in charge of the winds.

That means a sovereign God—who is both good and glorious—sits above the fray and his plans will always prevail, even when our plans don't.

This kind of thinking stretches our understanding and calls us to believe again that God is good and has good in mind for us, no matter what we see happening around us.

I think back to our May 2003 Passion Conference. Tens of thousands of college students and young adults were heading to a ranch property north of Dallas-Forth Worth to worship God and pray for their generation. That particular conference was going to be an outdoor event where people would camp in tents on the property. It was scheduled for two days and three nights. The day before the gathering officially started our team was on-site working feverishly to finish the final details.

The night before the majority of people were scheduled to arrive, thunder and lightning struck and threatened to blow all our plans apart. If you've ever lived in central Texas you know the storms come quickly and can be fierce. That night the rain fell with a fury. The storm sat directly on top of the ranch and wouldn't budge. We later discovered that the storm didn't show up as a potentially dangerous orange or red cell on the weather radar. A purple cell was overhead! It rained for eight hours straight, and in the morning, while it was still raining, we had to make a decision: cancel the conference or somehow go forward with it.

The ground was a quagmire, squishy to the point it would swallow your shoe or boot and not give it back as you pulled your foot away. You couldn't take a step on the property without a fight, much less drive a car on it. And this was before the era of social media and instant updates. We had no idea what to do.

So we prayed.

We prayed and prayed and prayed. In fact, that same first night just before the rain had begun to fall with such force, we'd gathered a group of our speakers and leaders and were praying in a huge tent for God to show up in power during OneDay 2003. Suddenly, the tent was getting sloshed by wind and rain and we started praying harder. We were calling for the wind and the waves to cease, but soon, we couldn't even hear ourselves, the storm was so loud. And we had all the spiritual heavyweights in that room praying with all the faith we could muster.

But the louder and harder we prayed, the louder and harder it stormed. Finally, one huge gust came along and lifted a portion of this massive tent on its poles and then lowered it back again. At that exact moment, a huge lightning bolt struck the ground maybe a hundred yards away from the tent. Thunder boomed in our ears like a cannon shot. Everybody ran for cover.

Including me.

Always God and Always Good

Sometimes life is like that.

You're living with good intentions, praying with all your heart, aiming for God's best, but the storm just blows harder, the rains keep falling. That can be really tough to deal with. Usually, the storm seems to be a sure sign God isn't with us. And often we actually think he may just be against us.

When you're in the midst of a storm, it's hard to remember that God is always good and glorious, and that God's plans will always prevail, even when yours don't.

Our RVs were set up some distance away from the main tent, and that's where we headed when we all ran. I felt so confused, so bewildered, so frustrated with what was happening; so disappointed.

Around midnight, the rain was still pelting the ground. I couldn't sleep. I knew the conference was doomed. My wife Shelley and I got down on the floor of our RV sometime early in the morning and wept. We literally sobbed. It felt like an entire year and a half's worth of work was destroyed. All of our hopes. All of our dreams. All of our finances. All of our prayers were being washed away. We just cried out to God, "Please, please let the storm pass." But all we heard was more rain pounding the top of our RV.

At 4 a.m. it was still raining.

At 5 a.m. it was still raining.

At 6 a.m. it was still raining.

At 7 a.m. it was still raining.

At 7:30 a.m. everybody was up, and we held another meeting.

During the night the tents of those already on-site were literally blown away or submerged in water. Lightning had struck one attendee, but fortunately they were going to be ok. Thousands waiting in their cars at the registration center were diverted in the night to a local high school gym. Who knows how many en route had turned back.

As our team met rain was still falling, but it looked to be slowing. Although the wind was still gusting hard. After a lot of prayer and discussion, we decided to go forward with the conference. Honestly, I'm not sure why. It was a gut decision. God had brought us this far. We were moving ahead.

By 5 p.m. that day, when the conference started, the rain had stopped, and cars were being driven onto the property twenty feet from the trailer where that meeting occurred at 7:30 a.m. And here's the amazing thing—the ground was as hard as a table. Thankfully, the ground was Texas sandy soil, and the same wind that had blown in the storm had also dried the ground. Some twenty-three thousand people eventually showed up. We prayed. We worshipped. We asked the God of heaven and earth to move mightily in this generation. And he did.

The fact that anybody was walking on that ground, much less driving on that ground, was a miracle. In our minds we looked upon that event as a "comeback"—what looked to have been a total wipeout turned out to be a life-altering event for this generation of Jesus followers.

Our plans were changed to God's plans, and God's plans were always for good.

Yet Again and Yet Again

Here are a couple of twists to the story.

After the conference was over, we took stock of any loose ends. Despite the large number of students who'd braved the weather and shown up anyway, thousands more had turned for home before they arrived thinking for sure the gathering was a no go. Without the ability to quickly update our website or tweet the latest info, people were left to their own conclusions.

In the end, the lower attendance cost us and we ended up with a financial shortfall. It wasn't any small shortfall either. We ended up being one hundred thousand dollars in the hole and we had little in the way of cash reserves. We'd never been in the hole like this before. We had no idea what we were going to do. It looked like we were sunk. What we needed was another comeback—and quick.

The Saturday following the conference, Shelley and I were at a wedding reception in Houston. A friend asked me how the conference ended up financially given the storm and I told him. He made one lap around the room, talked to a few people, came back, and told me that the one hundred thousand dollars we needed was secured; it would be wired to our offices on Monday.

Wow. We had no sooner told our board the good news when another crisis hit. What we hadn't figured, was even in spite of the money that had just come in, we still had payroll to meet, normal operating expenses, and the future to plan for. We needed another seventy-five thousand dollars—in about two weeks' time. We needed yet another comeback.

That day I got a call from a friend in Chicago who said, "Hey, this is kinda awkward, but I'm overnighting you a letter today that's been sitting on my desk for the past three weeks. I just moved a bunch of stuff on my desk and found it. Somehow it had gotten stuck under a pile. I'm really sorry about this. It was supposed to come in time for your conference. It's from our foundation and it includes a check for seventy-five thousand dollars."

Amazing, right?

How incredible that while we were praying and asking God to come through, yet again, he was looking at that check he had already provided hidden under a pile of stuff on my friend's desk.

Ready to Start Your Comeback Journey

Okay, so this is not a book about how to run a conference. It's not a book about finances. And it's not a book about how to manage a weather crisis.

This is a book about comebacks, about turnarounds, about fresh starts, and about new directions.

This is a book that describes how God always sees our needs right now, whatever our needs are, and how God's plans will always prevail.

Whatever problems we're going through, God already knows what the solutions are. No matter what kind of grief or pain or trouble or heartache we encounter, God can provide for our needs. Our problems might be spiritual, emotional, physical, mental, relational, financial, or directional. Whatever they are, God sees our need, and God comes through. He comes through in his time and in his way—he always comes through.

By sharing this opening story I'm certainly not trying to compare the potential cancellation of an event with the loss of your husband or wife, or child, or business, or sanity. What I'm saying is this: if your dreams have seemingly gone up in smoke, or in a sudden burst of wind and hail, don't count God out of the equation.

God's in the business of giving fresh starts to people. He gives hope to the hopeless, direction to the directionless, help for those who need help. He dries out the wet ground and blows away the storm clouds that threaten. God is always good, and God's plans will always prevail, even when our plans don't. Or when they need to be changed.

God is the God of the comeback, and if you're longing for some sort of a turnaround or fresh start or new direction, then this book's for you. It's a book of hope and help, encouragement and perspective. It's for you if you're feeling frustrated or confused, if you're in sorrow or in pain, if you're disappointed or feeling like life doesn't make sense. It's for you when you're discouraged or troubled or concerned about your life. Or maybe you just need a shot of encouragement. I think everyone feels that way from time to time.

In the pages ahead you'll see that, even when things look bleak, they may not turn out that way at all. You might be in tears on the floor of your RV, but help is at hand. Hold on until the morning. Hold on until the evening. Hold on for the next day. The wind that brought the storm will keep blowing. The ground will be solid and dry again, ready for whatever good God's prepared for you.

Your comeback is in God's plans right now.

—Louie Giglio
Atlanta, Georgia
July 2015

ONE

A DEEPER KIND OF COMEBACK STORY

Everyone loves a good comeback story.

Whether it's a touchdown in the final seconds of the fourth quarter, an impossible recovery from a terminal illness, a group of hostages released safely to the waiting arms of loved ones, or an amputated leg turned into an Olympic gold medal and a world record—we all love comeback stories. Somehow these stories strike a chord in the very core of our being. They make us realize that difficult circumstances do not always get the final say in our lives. They reveal to us that, in the end, our story can be a comeback story too.

Like this one. Maybe you remember this day. I know I do.

The ground shook on January 12, 2010. Buildings collapsed. A massive earthquake rocked the tiny country of Haiti. When the ground stopped shaking, thousands of buildings had been destroyed and some two hundred thousand people were dead.

When I first heard about this tragedy on the news, I couldn't get my mind around those numbers. It was too horrific, too catastrophic. The world responded with widespread humanitarian aid, yet it still felt like there was a gaping hole in the world.

Shelley and I had been to Haiti before the earthquake, and the country held a special place in our hearts. I couldn't imagine the pain and grief the people there were going through. I wondered if something more could be done, if there was some way I could enter their story along with them, even in the limited capacity of someone living in another country.

I came to know one man in particular: Ernst Leo, a thirty-five-year-old computer technician. He was at work in Port-au-Prince when the earthquake struck. He rushed home and found his home destroyed. The worst part was that his wife, Naomie, and his twelve-year-old daughter Faitza were buried in the debris of their collapsed apartment building. Both were dead. Ernst and Naomie had been sweethearts since childhood. Their seven-year-old daughter Therissa was still alive but trapped in the rubble.

For two days Ernst and rescue workers scrambled to free Therissa. Despite their efforts, she was hopelessly pinned beneath a massive concrete slab. Rescuers had no choice: they amputated her right arm to save her life.

When Therissa had healed enough from her wounds, she and her father moved into a tent in a refugee camp on a dead-end street near their destroyed home. All of their belongings fit into a small suitcase. They washed each night from a bucket. A massive restoration effort began across Haiti, but it was projected to take months, even years.

Ernst went back to work. Therissa went back to second grade. In the evenings the father and daughter sat together on broken cinder blocks while Ernst helped Therissa with her schoolwork. She learned to write with her left hand, but it was slow going. Such a great part of their lives had been ruined. Each day they fought to keep going while struggling with internal and external pain. This was their new reality—at the back of life's line.

Six months after the earthquake I hadn't yet met Ernst, and I didn't know his family, but their story pierced my heart. I was reading *USA Today* on an airplane, and the front-page article focused on Ernst and Therissa and how they were trying to rebuild their lives after the quake. Somehow I could get my mind around one man, one family. Ernst Leo was a middle-class guy just doing his job, loving his family, hoping to make a better way for those he loved most.

It was one of those moments when I couldn't move past the news. I felt face-to-face with this dad who'd lost a wife and a daughter. Face-to-face with this daughter who'd lost a mother, a sister, and an arm. I couldn't come close to solving Haiti's rebuilding challenges. But I could help this one man, this one family. I think I even said the words out loud, "I need to find this guy."

I made some calls and sent some e-mails and finally reached the writer of the newspaper story, who agreed to put me in touch with Ernst. A few weeks later I traveled to Haiti to meet Ernst and Therissa. For them the long-term answer lay in moving, and they were already working with relatives in Miami to immigrate to the United States. Ernst is hardworking and industrious. He wasn't looking for anybody to give him a handout. But he responded to the hand we extended to him, and he thanked us for playing a part in his comeback story.

We were able to help Ernst and Therissa get their own place in Miami and help furnish it. We helped to connect Ernst with churches in the area and bought him a used Camry to get to and from work and school. We found a specialist to fit Therissa with a prosthetic arm. At a Passion conference I told their story to university students who raised more than twenty-two thousand dollars for Therissa's college education. The help wouldn't bring back Naomie and Faitza. But it acted as a cup of cold water in the name of Jesus. I'd like to think it helped change the direction of their journey.

Looking back several years later, I now know why I responded to Ernst's story like I did. It's because I could see myself in his shoes. I could see myself sitting on a broken cinder block, hurting and grieving, wondering which way to go. I could see myself needing a comeback the same as Ernst had.

I've never lost loved ones in an earthquake. But I've experienced deep emotional and spiritual hurt. Low places in life. Times when I chose the wrong direction and needed to find my way back. Times when I wasn't sure how to overcome adversity. Can you relate?

I know a lot of us feel like that. We come to a place where we're walking through the fires and trials of life, and we don't know where to turn. What we need is a fresh start. We need our story to go in a new direction.

What we need is a comeback of our own.

The Start of Hope

The classic comeback story contains one of two twists. It's either about an underdog who falters and then succeeds beyond his dreams, or it's about a champion who falls, fights hard, and makes a big return.

Either way, it's about a person in pain whose pain is alleviated or who is able to see pain in a new perspective. There's a reversal of fortunes. Somebody was on the bottom and now he's on top. Or somebody was up against a great obstacle and now has overcome. Or someone does a dramatic about-face.

Great comeback stories give us hope. We can all relate to the experience of spending time in difficult places where we wondered if we were ever going to make it back. We all know what it feels like to have life disappoint us and not work out as we'd hoped. We've all been in seasons when we've longed for something better than what we're experiencing right now. We could all use a fresh start, a change of heart, or a powerful spiritual turnaround.

What kind of challenge are you facing today?

- Maybe you're facing conflict with your friends, coworkers, or relatives. Relationships are strained, and you don't know what to do. You need a comeback to renewed relationships.
- Maybe you're struggling to overcome an addiction or some sort of sin. You need a comeback from despair and darkness to victory, strength, and confidence.
- Perhaps you're overwhelmed at work. Or you hate your job. Or you can't find a job. Or you feel stuck in a dead-end job and it seems like there's no way forward. You need a fresh perspective, a new direction.
- Maybe you're going through a rough season academically, and you wonder if you're ever going to pass this course or graduate. You need a big dose of hope, an infusion of fresh strength.
- Perhaps a close relationship (perhaps your marriage) is on the rocks, and you wonder if you're going to make it through. You need to rekindle the love you once felt for each other.

- Maybe you have all the money and resources in the world, but your life feels empty and purposeless. You need a new purpose, a bigger purpose than you've ever had before.
- Maybe you're grieving deeply because of a great loss. Someone close to you has just died. Or something you once valued is no more. You need perspective in your pain. You need to journey forward in spite of your grief.
- Maybe you're in the midst of tragedy. There are no words to describe what you're going through. You just hurt. You need help taking your next breath.
- Maybe the problem is a serious and deep disappointment: life hasn't turned out for you the way you hoped it would. You're disillusioned or directionless. You want to know which way to go.

When a difficult season descends on us, sometimes we're there for a short time. But at other times it seems we find ourselves in that season for what seems like forever. Sometimes the end seems to be nowhere in sight. We long for a solution. We long to return to a place where an obstacle isn't a problem anymore.

The good news is that the life Jesus calls us all to enter is a life of comeback. On the one hand, it may be the kind of comeback where we overcome obstacles by God's power. On the other hand, it may be a deeper sort of comeback, where Jesus redeems the worst of circumstances for his glory and our best.

In this latter kind of comeback, maybe the problems we're wrestling with won't be solved—at least not in our lifetimes. Yet God offers us his presence in the middle of our problems. In his presence we find a deeper sort of solution, one that holds forth fulfillment, peace, a knowledge that he provides, and the hope that he has a wider purpose for our lives than we could ever think up or live out on our own.

The big hope ahead is that when we're at a low, God offers us a hand up. He holds forth a better way of living, a way filled with freedom, strength, peace, and Jesus. Through fires and trials, God offers us a closer walk with him.

Welcome to the Story of Us

Have you ever thought about this deeper sort of comeback—the kind of comeback that only God can offer? God offers this comeback to everybody. Just think of some of the remarkable comeback stories in the Bible.

In the story about the garden of Eden in Genesis 2–3, Adam and Eve in paradise had everything they needed. Yet they failed miserably when they ate the forbidden fruit. They needed a comeback. Their problem was that they had believed a lie that many of us believe even today: they thought God was withholding something good from them, so they chose to go in a harmful direction, a direction that was clearly off-limits.

In his grace and mercy, God appeared to Adam and Eve in the midst of their failure. Yes, they suffered the consequences of their sin, and yes, the whole world has experienced those consequences ever since, thanks to Adam and Eve, because we're all in this together. But the mercy of God also came into the garden in a big way, and Adam and Eve experienced a comeback and went on to have a hope and a future and a great story with God. Even after their failure, God did not abandon them. Quite the opposite—God loved them, cared for them, blessed them, and sustained them.

We've all heard the story of Noah's ark in Genesis 6–9. Noah built a big boat, gathered all the animals inside two by two, and also saved a remnant of humanity from complete destruction during a worldwide flood. It's a story we like to tell children because it features fuzzy animals, a rainbow, and a happy ending. But there's more to that story and it's not all nice.

Right after Noah and his family were saved, they climbed out of the boat onto dry ground under a fantastic rainbow. But one of the next things Noah did was plant a vineyard and get drunk. Sure, he saved the world, but Noah also had a major drinking problem, and his actions caused big conflict in his family. Fortunately, that's not all there is to Noah's story. Hebrews 11 describes how Noah became an heir of righteousness in keeping with his faith. Noah had a comeback, and God used Noah powerfully, even after his mistakes.

Abraham's story is told in Genesis 12–23, and he's considered the father of our faith, but he had a waiting problem to the point that he gave up on the promise of God. A son was promised to him, a promise that was renewed when Abraham was an old man. Abraham had wanted a son his whole life. He wanted this son more than anything else in the world. But year after year passed, and no baby was born.

So Abraham tried to make God's plan happen on his own by fathering a child with a maidservant. This wasn't God's idea, and Abraham messed up the plan, yet God still had mercy on him. When Abraham was a hundred years old, his wife gave birth to the promised son, Isaac, who eventually had descendants as numerous as the stars in the sky. Abraham bailed out on God's plan, but there was a comeback for Abraham, and he was blessed for his faith.

In Exodus, the story of Moses is told. Moses had an anger problem and killed an Egyptian who was beating a Hebrew slave. Moses took matters into his own hands the only way he knew how, yet a crime was still a crime, and because of that crime, Moses needed to leave Pharaoh's house, where he'd grown up. Moses was banished to the wilderness, where all he did for years was tend sheep.

Far away from anything, in the backside of life and in the middle of nowhere, a bush caught fire and blazed without burning up. From that burning bush God spoke to Moses and said, "Take heart! I know it looks like life has passed you by, but I'm going to use you to lead my people out of bondage in Egypt and into the Promised Land."

Moses had a great comeback story over his anger and failed opportunities. But he also had a speech impediment and lousy self-confidence. He didn't think he could do anything useful for God, but along with his brother, Aaron, he went to Pharaoh and told him to let God's people go. Eventually Pharaoh did that, and the whole nation had a comeback story.

Moses had relapses and disobeyed God a few times after that, and God wouldn't let him go into the Promised Land as a consequence. But in the New Testament, there's a story of Jesus hiking up on a mountain with two of his disciples. There something supernatural happened. Jesus' clothes turned a radiant white, and he shone in brilliant glory in the presence of his disciples. Alongside Jesus two others suddenly appeared, and one of them was Moses, in his all-time most powerful comeback. In the grace of God there is a comeback for people who've already had a comeback and need another.

We could talk about story after story like these. In fact, the entire story of humanity is a story of people who have stumbled and fallen, yet somehow in this ocean of God's grace and mercy, he provides a comeback for anyone who puts their faith and hope in Jesus.

That's what this book is about. In the pages ahead we're going to explore the stories of men and women who have gone through the fires and trials of life and come out believing in the faithfulness and grace of God. These stories show us that no matter what we might be walking through, we can still have confidence that Jesus is the God of the comeback and that our story is not over as long as Jesus is in it.

Everybody needs a comeback, and if we seek God everybody is offered a comeback. No matter what our obstacles are, no matter what mistakes we've made, no matter if we're in a season of wandering or darkness, God's purpose and plan will still prevail.

God is all about restoring us—sometimes now, sometimes in heaven. God has the ability to do anything at any time to restore anything that's been lost. Even if something doesn't look restored now on earth, we're invited to have confidence in God's purposes, and that yields hope and peace for us today.

I know this to be true because I've experienced a comeback personally.

A Song in the Night

A few years back, life was pumping. In a six-month span, Passion hosted events in seventeen global cities. It was one of the most amazing experiences of my life. Yet it also required an enormous amount of leadership and courage, and the toll was greater than

I thought. Add to the mix, we were planting a church in Atlanta and dealing with massively challenging circumstances that were swirling around our family. The world economy hit bottom. And, ultimately, so did I.

One morning at 2 a.m., completely out of nowhere, I woke up with a jolt and sat straight up in bed. Sweat was building on my forehead. My heart was racing like nothing I'd experienced before. I thought it might blow out of my chest. And I thought this is what it must feel like when you die.

I got up out of bed and tried to walk it off, eventually washing my face with cold water in the bathroom. I tried to calm myself down, but couldn't. I held on till morning, but not much had changed. Sitting at my desk at work, I felt another wave coming on and eventually headed to my doctor.

The short story is that I was back in the ER that same night with convulsions, random numbness, intense pains, and other crazy symptoms. As Shelley drove me to St. Joseph's Hospital in the middle of the night, we were quiet. Perplexed. Afraid. Bewildered.

I said to the person at the ER desk, "I'm fifty and I can't feel my face." I found out that will get you past the waiting room line. Immediately I was hooked up to multiple machines and the tests began. My blood pressure was so high you wouldn't believe me if I told you. Scans followed. Then nothing.

The attending doctor came in and said, "Your heart is fine. You don't have any signs of major illness." And then he left.

Interestingly, my blood pressure began to drop, starting a cycle that would repeat for weeks to come. The meds he gave me instantly calmed me down and I was able to sleep that night. But what I didn't know was underneath it all something was wrong. Something was broken inside me that wasn't going to reset quickly or easily.

The 2 a.m. wake-ups kept coming. The symptoms changed day to day, but persisted. My vision blurred. And every day I thought I was dying from a new ailment.

Yet, visit after visit to doctor after doctor found nothing. Every test turned up negative, and I do mean every test possible.

No one could say what was wrong. All the doctors were doing was crossing off what *wasn't wrong*. Finally, someone said the word: *depression*. Some kind of anxiety disorder had taken hold of the control center in my mind. The panic attacks and random symptoms were the fruit. The depression was the root. But how do you fix it?

I was stuck in a pattern of 2 a.m. dread. No matter when I went to sleep, the early morning cloud of dread would come. I'd sense the internal *boom*, sit up in bed and feel the darkness hanging overhead. Closing in.

By now I was taking medication to reset my brain, but night after night after night the dread and darkness would come calling. It's hard to explain unless you've been there, but in a moment like this you feel the pit is deep and you're never coming back.

Of course I had prayed. And the people around me who knew what was really going on had been praying for months. Yet I was feeling numb from the meds and lost in the fog. Finally, one night something changed.

I'll never forget the 2 a.m. *boom* that night and waking up feeling more desperate than ever. I thought, *I can't do this anymore.* Nothing had helped the situation. No doctor was able to bring about a change. I didn't know what to do. All I knew for certain was that I couldn't go on this way.

I was at the bottom.

Almost on reflex, I felt my arms rising to heaven. Without words, my heart prayed, *God, you've got to help me.* That's all I could muster. Sometimes our best and most profound prayers are the simplest. All I was saying was, *God, please help me.*

There was no bolt of lightning. No fast fix. No immediate cure.

But the smallest snippet of Scripture floated through my mind. It's from the book of Job (35:10) and talks about how God gives us songs in the night. Worship had been my go-to many times before in life when the night was the darkest and I said, *God, I don't know what else to do, but if you'll give me a song in the dark, I will praise you.*

Almost instantly this little line of praise to God just dropped into my mouth. It was, "Be still, my soul, there's a healer." And I thought, *Okay, I'll sing that.* That's all I had. "Be still, my soul, there's a healer." I sang it over and over again, a little melody emerging in my mouth. I knew the truth of that line. I knew it deep in my gut. I knew it was backed up by Scripture. The Psalmist said: "Why are you cast down, O my soul, and why are you in turmoil within me? Hope in God; for I shall again praise him, my salvation and my God" (43:5). *Put your hope in God.*

Have you ever experienced a moment like that? Maybe you're good at giving advice to your friends but not so good at giving advice to yourself. I'm that way. Times come in life when you're on your own and you're at some kind of dead end. You're in the middle of darkness and going through the valley of the shadow of death, and in that moment you need to start proclaiming the living Word of God to yourself. You face yourself in the mirror and deliver your best messages, reminding yourself of the truths in the Bible.

That's what that little line was to me. *Be still, my soul, there's a healer.* There, in the darkness, God didn't heal me instantly. The little song wasn't a promise that God would heal me then and there, and he might not heal me the next day either. Yet God was still a healer, and I believed in him and in his purposes, and that was enough for the moment. That's what I needed to remind myself of.

And then more words came.

His love is deeper than the sea. His mercy is unfailing. His arms a fortress for the weak.

I sang it again. I kept singing it over and over.

What happened the next morning? Was everything all okay with me?

Nope.

The next night 2 a.m. came and the same thing happened: I sat straight up in bed, wide-awake with my heart racing, and feeling a huge sense of dread. A cloud of darkness descended over me. But one thing was different that night: I had a song.

The next night was the same. First the cloud, then the song.

The night after that, my pattern alternated: cloud, song, cloud, song.

The night after that, I woke up on my own before 2 a.m. I was prepared for the cloud. That night the order was song, cloud, song, cloud.

For nights, weeks, and even months to come, I experienced a strange rhythm of dread and peace, peace and dread. Some nights it was cloud, cloud, song, song. Other nights it was song, song, cloud, cloud.

Gradually, mercifully, it became song, song, song, cloud.

Then one night it became song, song, song, song. No cloud at all.

Then, tentatively, the next night it was song, song, song, song.

For weeks and months on end it remained simply song, song, song, song.

An Invitation to Raise Your Hands

Yes, I had the help of a doctor during that season of recovery. I made lifestyle changes. I required medications for a season. It all helped. Yet I know it was the song of praise that pierced the deepest heart of that darkness to provide the comeback I needed. The song of praise opened up the path that led me through that valley and back to the light of day.

So, has that ever happened since, you ask? In the spirit of full disclosure, I have struggled with that sense of panic to varying degrees in the years that have followed. But I know what I am up against and have learned how to think/believe my way above the cloud when it tries to creep back into the story. Praise God, I have never gone back to that debilitating place.

I want to say two things to anybody who feels they're in a dark place: you're not crazy and you're not alone. Your circumstances may be black, but Scripture says that God is light. Trust in him, and he will give you a comeback. He will give you a fresh start. He will give you a change of heart and provide a powerful spiritual turnaround. He is with you in the midst of the valley of the shadow of death, and I invite you to praise him and trust his purposes for your life.

Life deals us blows, yes. Circumstances come up that are beyond our control, and obstacles keep us from living the life that we dream of. Sometimes we deal blows to ourselves. We make mistakes and wrong decisions and choose paths that are harmful, not helpful.

But there is hope.

Over the next several chapters, I'm going to share some incredible comeback stories and pray that the Holy Spirit breathes life into them. The premise I want to raise in your mind is this: *I need a comeback.* The question I want to raise in your mind is this: *How do I get one?*

Part of the beautiful solution I can offer you, even now, is that the solution isn't about your trying harder. When people read books by preachers or hear talks at church and similar places, too often the solution points to something you need to do to change. You need to walk forward or backward or commit yourself to fifty days of something or light a candle or put a stick in the fire. But then no lasting change comes, and you wonder what you did wrong.

The solution I'm pointing you to is a solution of faith. It's not a formula, but there is real evidence that it works. The solution lies in a relationship with Jesus Christ.

The Psalmist described the need for a big comeback: "Oh God, you are my God; earnestly I seek you; my soul thirsts for you; my flesh faints for you, as in a dry and weary land where there is no water" (Psalm 63:1).

Those are the words of a man who's in a place of turmoil. Then the Psalmist remembered to have faith. He said to God:

> *So I have looked upon you in the sanctuary,*
> *beholding your power and glory.*
> *Because your steadfast love is better than life,*
> *my lips will praise you. (63:2–3)*

And here comes the comeback. Here comes the song in the night. The Psalmist said: "I will bless you as long as I live" (v. 4). Does that sound like a strange solution to you?

If you need a comeback, the solution I'm pointing you to begins with praise. This might sound like something that's only for deeply spiritual people or for those who appear to have it all together. But that's not how it works. I know people can be all over the map spiritually. Maybe you're reading this book and you don't know God at all. Or maybe God seems like he's far off. Maybe you knew God when you were younger, but that seems like a long time ago. Or maybe you just want God to feel closer than he seems right now. All of that is okay.

When you lift your hands in praise, you're acknowledging that someone exists who's greater than you. You believe that same someone is reaching down with an outstretched hand, and you're responding to him in faith. You don't need to have all the answers at first. If you want a comeback, then Acts 16:31 invites you with one straightforward declaration: "Believe in the Lord Jesus, and you will be saved."

That's what hands lifted in praise to God represent. You see hands lifted in praise both in times of jubilant celebration and in times of desperate hope. You see it all over humanity everywhere. Think about those times when you're watching the news and hear about an earthquake that has wiped out a city or a tsunami that has slammed into people's lives and they're wondering how to begin again. In the middle of the devastation, what do you see?

You see people's hands lifted to heaven, crying out. It's the way humans respond when they don't know where else to turn. They think, *Someone help me.*

That's the invitation this book holds out to you.

You might be in a dry and weary land right now, but yes, you can praise God.

You might be in the valley of the shadow of death, but yes, you can praise God.

You might have just received a prognosis with news you didn't expect, but yes, you can praise God.

You might be running headlong into a strong wind, where a storm is blasting straight against your face, but with all the breath left in your lungs, you can praise God.

The comeback God offers you starts right now. Lift up your hands in response to God's reaching down to you. Lift your hands in praise above the darkness, above death and the grave, above cancer, above loss, above a bad job situation, above a strained relationship, above depression or turmoil or stress or whatever it is that has come against you.

Lift them up to believe again and to declare that although God has led you into this valley, his plan is not to leave you in this place but to give you a comeback and lead you all the way through.

TWO

PARADISE IN A GARBAGE DUMP

One day Rachel woke up with a gun to her head. She didn't know how she got there or why someone was pointing a gun at her. She just knew she was in trouble. In a desperate mess.

It didn't happen overnight. Years earlier, when Rachel was about twelve, her stepfather lost a battle with methamphetamines and went on a downward spiral. The family fell apart. Rachel's mom spent so much time trying to take care of the family's immediate needs for food, clothing, and shelter that she didn't have a lot of time for anything else.

A decade passed and someone introduced Rachel to the club scene when she was about twenty-two. Immediately she was enthralled. Usually she felt tremendously insecure, but the men at the clubs told her that she was beautiful. They bought her drinks and gave her presents, and she was intrigued because it felt like she was finally finding the love and acceptance she so desperately craved.

Rachel's life began to head down a dark path. One problem led to another. One drink led to another. One man led to another. One drug led to another. None of it ever filled the deep pain and longing in her heart. There were mornings when her five-year-old son needed to take care of her because she couldn't get out of bed. She was so miserably hungover.

The day she woke up with a gun to her head, she somehow got out of that desperate situation and realized she had reached the bottom. Life felt completely hopeless. The idea for a plan of action that the gun had introduced began to look good. Rachel asked herself, *Why not just go ahead and end your life?*

That day, on the way to work, Rachel said she kept trying to get the courage to drive her car off the road and hopefully end it all. When she arrived at the club, she was so frustrated that she didn't have the guts to take her life. Rather than face another night in a world she had grown to despise, Rachel gathered her belongings before her shift started and began to leave with thoughts of taking another run at ending her life.

As Rachel was preparing to leave, a group of ladies from the nearby church came in. One of those ladies, noticing Rachel was very upset and emotional, approached her to see if she could help. The woman had come before, with permission from the club manager, and shared gifts with the girls, looked after their needs, and prayed for them. But Rachel was furious. First the failure to end her life, and now the ladies from the church!

"You're from the church, right?" she blurted.

"Yes, I am," the woman responded, stating the obvious.

"Well," Rachel started in, "Let me tell you about my life."

For the next few minutes, Rachel unloaded. Her hurt and pain spilled out without restraint. Her anger uncorked, she recounted all the abuse and darkness and abandonment and darkness. Finally, her story was laid bare and she locked eyes with the woman.

Through tears mixed with cutting sarcasm, she asked, "So, what do you and your God have to say about all that?"

The woman looked back at Rachel with tears welling in her eyes. She could see the toll the years had taken on her heart and she gently replied, "Rachel, thank you so much for trusting me with your story. I'm so, so sorry that happened to you."

No sermon. No pious reply. No high horse. No bumper sticker quote. Just compassion.

The woman's words, drenched in God's grace, broke Rachel's hardened approach and they began to talk. They talked about Jesus. But Rachel felt ashamed, like Jesus could never love her. She was an exotic dancer. She was a drug addict. She was an alcoholic. And she was a self-admitted horrible mother. Her questions sounded huge: "How could Jesus ever love me? How could Jesus ever be proud of me? How could Jesus call me his daughter when I feel so unworthy?"

Jesus meets people exactly where they are. Have you ever thought about that? I mean, Jesus meets people anywhere!

Let that one word sink in. ANYWHERE.

That same night, Jesus scooped Rachel up out of the darkness and gave her light and hope and a future. Today, Rachel's life looks very different than it did a couple of years ago. She's no longer working as an exotic dancer. Drugs and alcohol no longer rule her life. Jesus is healing her wounds day-by-day. She has completed a long-term rebuilding program and moved to a new city where she lives with a family who loves her and her son, and is modeling the fullness of Jesus' love for her.

It's not an easy road. Rachel has a lot to learn and unlearn from years of brokenness. But Rachel is sober, sane, and alive. She's a symbol of hope for other women stranded in her former situation. She's on her way to becoming a better parent. God has given her a fresh start. Recently her son said to her, "Mom, I just love the new you, and I'm so glad you're better."

Rachel's story is more than an illustration in a book. She is a real person who matters to God. I will never, ever forget the day she was baptized in our church and shared her story with us all. Rachel has a second chance and is on a new path by the power of God's Spirit in her.

That's all because of Jesus.

A Comeback Tailor-Made for You

Not all of us have stories as extreme as Rachel's. But no matter the pain we're going through or the distance we've traveled away from God, Jesus is always there for us. He doesn't stop healing us. He never stops forgiving us. He won't stop restoring us. He refuses to stop loving us.

What kind of comeback are you hoping for?

I don't know the specific circumstances of your life, but maybe you want a comeback because you've really stumbled along the way. Maybe you did something that embarrassed you or a whole lot of people. Or maybe it was more serious. Maybe you gave in to a moral weakness. Or you said something that ruined a relationship. Or maybe your actions drove a wedge between you and what was right. Maybe you're just exhausted and burned out. Your life feels chaotic and out of control. You want a fresh start but you don't know what to do or where to turn.

We've all been there. We've all experienced times of trouble, from outside ourselves and from inside. We've all fallen short of the glory of God over and over again. In times like those, our feelings may range from anger and denial to heaping shame on ourselves, to discouragement and hopelessness, to remorse and regret, to purposelessness, and to pure pain. We wonder if things will ever be good again. We wonder if we'll ever find a way forward.

Fortunately, there's good news. Whatever our individual story is, our story joins a larger story: a story of people who have stumbled and fallen, a story of people whose lives were messy, a story of people whose lives were broken and confused, yet they were invited to experience the ocean of God's love.

There's a strong comeback picture in the classic C. S. Lewis book *The Lion, the Witch and the Wardrobe*. As the story goes, the White Witch had inflicted perpetual winter on the land but never allowed Christmas. Narnia was gripped in the bleakest ice and snow, a great hardship to all the little animal-people of the land. The children—Susan, Peter, and Lucy—are fleeing with Mr. and Mrs. Beaver from the White Witch when they hear sleigh bells and think she has caught up with them in her white sleigh. But it turns out to be Father Christmas, bringing gifts and saying, "She has kept me out for a long time, but I have got in at last. Aslan is on the move. The Witch's magic is weakening."[1]

Aslan, you remember, is the lion who symbolizes Jesus in the story. From this point on, the land begins to experience a thaw. The boy Edmund has been captured by the White Witch because of his fascination with a particularly tempting candy known as Turkish Delight. He's now a hostage forced to race through the woods in the witch's sleigh. Edmund notices it's becoming warmer, and he hears "a sweet, rustling, chattering noise . . . the noise of running water. All round them, though out of sight,

---

1 C. S. Lewis, *The Lion, the Witch and the Wardrobe* (New York: HarperCollins, c. 1950, 1994 edition), 117.

there were streams, chattering, murmuring, bubbling, splashing and even (in the distance) roaring."[2] Soon there are the plops of snow sliding off fir branches, patches of green grass, birdsong, trees beginning to leaf out. "Coming suddenly round a corner into a glade of silver birch trees, Edmund saw the ground covered in all directions with little yellow flowers."[3] A dwarf tells the White Witch, "This is no thaw. This is spring. Your winter has been destroyed, I tell you! This is Aslan's doing."[4]

What Aslan was doing for Narnia is exactly what Jesus does for our spirits. He melts the grip of sin and dire circumstances and leads us back to his springtime full of life and growth, productivity and beauty.

The good news is that this kind of comeback is available for everyone who puts his faith and hope in Jesus. Everyone needs a comeback. And everyone who wants a comeback receives a comeback. That's the shape our story begins to take: from winter to spring.

In the last chapter, we talked about how, if we want a comeback, the place to begin is with lifted hands of praise. It's important to know who we're praising, because it isn't just anybody or anything. We're not praising trees or rocks or Mother Nature. Who we're praising is much closer and much more glorious, because we're praising a person, one who is both intimate and ultimate. He is the giver of comebacks and he leads us in our personal, tailor-made comeback journey.

That person is Jesus. He's the God of all comebacks. And within your comeback journey, I invite you to get to know him well.

---

2 Ibid., 129.
3 Ibid., 131.
4 Ibid., 133.

Please, Just Remember Me

Jesus wasn't drawn to the people whose lives were perfectly put together. (Actually, those people never existed.) Jesus was drawn to people whose lives *weren't* all together. People just like us. In fact, some of the people he interacted with were a real mess.

Think about the story of the thief on the cross. The events leading up to it include Jesus willingly giving himself up for the sins of the world, his being rushed through a series of injustices, and his crucifixion on a Roman cross. That's where things took a twist, because other people became closely associated in the crucifixion account of Jesus. Two of them hung on crosses alongside him. We see this in Luke 23:32–33 (NIV).

> Two other men, both criminals, were also led out with him to be executed. When they came to the place called the Skull, they crucified him there, along with the criminals—one on his right, the other on his left.

Did you catch that?

In Jesus' last hours on earth, God chose to put Jesus in close proximity to two really messed-up people. As Jesus hung dying on the cross, on his right and on his left were two other people on crosses. These two were common criminals. Three men were crucified that day. Not one. Why's that important? Because God wants us to remember that there's always a connection between the ministry of Jesus and ordinary people who are at the end of their rope.

We don't know much about these criminals. They're identified as thieves, but we don't know what they stole or how much. In Jesus' time, the law of the land meant the laws of the Roman

Empire, and the Romans had a low tolerance for any crime, particularly in the countries they conquered. Even petty theft could be cause for capital punishment.

The location of the crucifixion also was key. It was common for a person to be crucified near a busy road, where passersby could see the punishment up close and personal. Those who traveled along the road would shake their heads and mutter, "I don't know what those guys did, but I want to make sure I don't ever do anything close to it."

Luke's gospel records how passersby watched Jesus and the thieves as the three were being crucified. Some sneered at Jesus and mocked him. "He saved others," they said, "let him save himself" (23:35). They didn't realize that Jesus was giving his innocent life for the sins of the world. Jesus knew he had the power to blow up the moment. Any time he wanted to, he could jump off that cross and be perfectly fine. But he hung there silently, yielding to the purpose for which he had come.

One of the criminals hanging alongside Jesus hurled taunts at him. Undoubtedly, that thief had been deeply wounded somewhere along the road of life. His pain led him to despair, and despair led to crime. In his last moments of life, as his last act in the world, he chose to wound another person by doing the only thing he could think to do: insult him.

The way a crucifixion went down is that they nailed you to a wooden cross and you hung there by the spikes driven through your hands and feet. The weight of your body caused your chest to sag, which put enormous pressure on your lungs. The only way you could breathe was to push up against the nails in your feet to lift your body up enough so you could take a quick gulp of air. Eventually the pain raced through your body and exhausted you until you no longer had the strength to push up and breathe. Sometimes you would die by blood loss, if your earlier beatings had been severe enough, but usually a person died by suffocation. Depending on what physical shape you were in, you might hang on a cross for days, gasping for air. If your death took that long, eventually a soldier would break your shins. You'd no longer have the ability to push yourself up to breathe, so you'd die more quickly.

Picture the thief who was flinging insults at Jesus. He only had a few breaths left, but he was using all his strength to lift himself up so he could gasp for air and spit out some final words of insult to someone else. That was how much pain he was in. His life was so full of hatred and hurt that insulting others had become his default action, even in his last few moments of life.

Some of us today understand what it's like to hurt that much. We're not being crucified on a cross, but we know how it feels to hate others. So many wounds have been inflicted on us over the years that all we know how to do is to strike back. Wounding others has become our defense mechanism. Retaliation has become our form of self-preservation. We think that by wounding others, somehow we'll stay safe. That's what this criminal on the cross was doing.

But here's a contrast. There were two criminals on the crosses beside Jesus. One was insulting Jesus. Guess what the other criminal was doing? Luke records his actions.

But the other rebuked him, saying, "Do you not fear God, since you are under the same sentence of condemnation? And we indeed justly, for we are receiving the due reward of our deeds; but this man has done nothing wrong." (23:40–41)

I would love to know if more words followed. We know that none of the four Gospels record every detail that happened at the cross. We have to weave the four accounts together to get the full picture. Maybe other things were said that weren't recorded at all. If I'd been that guy, I would have turned to the scornful thief and said, "Will you just shut up? What are you thinking?! Here we are at the end of our lives, and you're hurling insults at God! It might have been easy to insult God when we were out stealing on the streets and hadn't been caught. But here on these crosses, we are not in charge! Today we're going to die, and you're telling me you don't even fear God now?"

The second thief understood the gravity of the moment. He got it. Maybe he'd heard Jesus teach earlier, or maybe he'd seen Jesus do a miracle. He had somehow connected the dots. He understood so deeply what Jesus was about that in Luke 23:42, the thief's final recorded words are this poignant plea: "Jesus, remember me when you come into your kingdom." A nine-word prayer. It wasn't a grand theological statement, and it might have been the only prayer this thief ever prayed in his life, yet it demonstrated that he had a clear view in his heart of who Jesus was and what Jesus was capable of doing.

Have you ever prayed a similar prayer?

Jesus, please remember me.

Isn't that really what all of us are hoping for today? A person who prays, *Jesus, please remember me,* is a person who needs a comeback. The prayer is that somehow God hasn't forgotten us in this crazy world. Although we may be completely lost in despair and darkness and winter without Christmas, God holds out hope that we may come back to him. Even though our marriage might have hit rock bottom, there's still a chance the mediation is going to work. God hasn't forgotten us. Or even though we've made a huge mistake that's resulted in a complete mess, there's still hope. That's the heart of a powerful prayer from a heart that desperately needs God. *God, please don't forget me. God, please remember me.*

The great news is that Jesus met the praying thief exactly where he was. Luke records Jesus' answer to the thief: "Truly, I say to you, today you will be with me in Paradise" (23:43). That's a great comeback story.

How did this thief know to trust Jesus so intently? We're not quite sure. In other places in Scripture, Jesus is recorded throwing into his conversations little snippets about his resurrection to come, and maybe the thief had heard one of those.

For instance, right after Peter made his grand statement that he'd never deny Jesus, the Lord turned to Peter and told him that Peter would deny him before the rooster crowed. Right after that, Jesus added, "But after I am raised up, I will go before you to Galilee" (Matthew 26:32).

Jesus often tucked in little phrases like that. Continually, throughout his ministry on earth, he was letting people know that hope was on its way.

He said things such as this:

My body will be broken for you and my blood spilled for many for the forgiveness of sins, yet one of you is going to betray me. In fact, all of you are going to let me down. That's what this is about. You are going to fall, but I'm going to do a great work to raise you up. I am Jesus, and my story is a comeback story. I'm going to be crucified, dead, and buried, yes. I'm going to carry the guilt and shame of the world. But

God the Father is going to call my name and raise me up. I'm going to beat the grave, beat darkness and death, beat sin and all its penalty, beat hell itself. I'm coming back out of death to live again to be seated at God's right hand in the position of authority.

That's what the thief acknowledged on the cross. Maybe he didn't use all of those words. Maybe he only had enough facts to know that Jesus was God and that Jesus had the power to remember him. What's important for us to know is this: three men died that day, and two went to paradise.

That's a great comeback story.

Welcome to the Garbage Dump

At the risk of being overly graphic, here's something you need to know about where Jesus was crucified. Historians and archaeologists tell us that the little section of land called Golgotha, where Jesus was crucified, was actually a landfill.

Have you ever seen a landfill up close? Flies buzzing around. A bad smell in the air. Everywhere you look is pile after pile of rotting, stinking trash. And Golgotha was the worst sort of primitive, barbaric landfill possible.

When the Romans were crucifying criminals, often there'd be nobody around afterward to claim the bodies. Nobody wanted anything to do with folks who'd been in trouble with the law. So the soldiers would peel the bodies off the beams and toss the corpses into the garbage heap. Then the wild dogs and other feral animals on the outskirts of the city would eat the flesh off the bones. No costly elaborate burials were necessary. That's the place where Jesus was crucified—the worst sort of garbage dump imaginable.

The fact that Jesus told the thief on the cross that he would be with Jesus in paradise is highly significant for you and me today. You see, on that day, paradise came to a landfill. Paradise was connected to a garbage dump. The connection was Jesus. We may be living in a garbage dump today, but paradise can still find us. Our lives may be disgustingly messy and flies may buzz all around us, but Jesus is always near. That's great news, because even if we're in a really tough spot, we never need to count ourselves out. There's always hope. If the life of someone we know looks completely messed up, we don't need to count that person out. God is the God of the great comeback.

How does a great comeback begin? It springs from simple faith from a heart that believes enough to pray a basic prayer: *Jesus, please remember me.* That prayer only requires a breath, just enough to change the direction of our eternity. God placed the criminal in proximity to Jesus because God wanted to let us know we don't need to be high and mighty to get to heaven. We aren't blessed by God because we're better than anyone else. We get to heaven because of a simple prayer of faith.

In that prayer we acknowledge that we have nothing to offer God. We come to Jesus as helpless in our pain and despair as a thief stretched out on a cross. We look at Jesus on the cross beside us and say, "You're God. You're innocent of any crimes. You could get down off that cross if you wanted, but you're there by choice for a purpose. Will you please remember me?"

Sometimes people put more words around that prayer—and that's fine. You might understand more about spiritual matters than the thief did. Maybe you grew up around Scripture and you know we've all sinned and fallen short of the glory of God (Romans 3:23). Maybe you know that the wages of sin is death (Romans 6:23), but Christ came to take away our sin (1 John 3:5), and his sacrifice removes the stain of our sin (Hebrews 9:28). You know that in him we are born to a brand-new life by his Spirit (John 3:6). You know that his Holy Spirit comes into our hearts and brings our spirits to life (1 Thessalonians 3:8). You know we are reborn as sons and daughters of God (2 Corinthians 6:18). You know now that you have the power of God to walk in faith and to live out the hope of God for your life (Romans 1:16). That's wonderful if you know those things.

But if you know far less, that's okay too. If all you know is that Jesus was innocent, crucified for things he didn't do but things that you had a part in doing, and if you believe that Jesus could have climbed off that cross if he wanted to but stayed there for a reason, and you just want Jesus to remember you, then your prayer is heard.

God will hear your simple prayer and bring paradise to the messiest situations and lives. Jesus is not afraid of darkness. He's not put off by the stench of old rotten bones.

Jesus will bring paradise even to a garbage dump.

It's Never Too Late

Think about this line: *comeback begins with Jesus.* Does that seem too simple for you?

We often think we need to do something great ourselves in order to have a comeback. We need to jump high hurdles or climb ladders to heaven. At the very least, we mistakenly think we need to be in the right place at the right time.

The good news is that the essential action has nothing to do with us. In fact, when it comes to being in position, it's only important that Jesus is in the right place at the right time. And you can count on him not to miss his cue. Do you think that the thief on the cross said to himself, *Wow, how fortunate I am to be crucified today! I mean, here I am, hanging right next to Jesus of Nazareth. What luck!* Of course not. It wasn't about the thief's being in the right place at the right time; it was about Jesus coming to be beside him.

There are so many stories in the Bible that show how Jesus is always on time and in the right place, ready to bring his greatness into any situation.

Once there was a little girl who became very sick. Her story is told in Luke 8:40–56. Her dad went after Jesus and finally found him, but Jesus was delayed and didn't get back to the man's house in time. By the time Jesus arrived, the little girl was dead.

But even then it wasn't too late for that little girl. I mean, that poor child was truly dead. The mourners had arrived. The flute players were out. The blinds were closed. But Jesus said, "Don't worry—she's not dead. She's only sleeping." He went into the room where the little girl lay and told her to wake up. And the little girl opened her eyes! The father was like, "Wow!" And the mourners said, "I guess we're not getting paid today."

It wasn't too late for the girl and her family, because Jesus is the God of the comeback.

Once there was a woman who'd been sick for many years (her story is told in the same passage). No doctor could help her. She knew she needed to get close to Jesus and he would heal her.

But there were huge crowds around Jesus. Getting close to him seemed impossible, and I imagine she was growing weaker by the minute.

But it wasn't too late for her.

All she did was reach out and touch the hem of his garment as he passed by, just a finger brushing lightly against the edge of his robe.

Jesus knew that power had gone out from him. He said, "Daughter, stand up, your faith has made you whole." Immediately the woman was healed.

It wasn't too late for that woman, because Jesus is the God of the comeback.

Luke 19:1–10 tells the story of a man who worked for the government who'd been involved in some shady business dealings. He was the chief tax collector for the city of Jericho. People knew about his dealings and hated him. The man knew he needed help, but who was ever going to help a corrupt businessman? He desperately wanted to see Jesus. He wanted Jesus to come to his home so they could talk in private. But there was another problem: the man was really short and Jesus was always surrounded by crowds. The man simply couldn't see over the heads of the other people. Getting close to Jesus seemed impossible, and inviting Jesus to his house seemed out of the question.

But it wasn't too late for that man.

Just before Jesus passed along his street, the businessman climbed a sycamore tree. And when Jesus came to that spot, he stopped and looked right into the man's face. Before the man could get out a word, Jesus called him by name. "Zacchaeus!" he said, "come down from that tree. I'm going to your house today."

Everybody in the crowd was shocked that Jesus would go

to the house of a tax collector. Tax collectors were known to be cheats and scam artists. But Jesus didn't care. And right then and there, Zacchaeus' heart was healed. He realized that money would never satisfy the truest longings of his heart, and he vowed to give half of his possessions to the poor and pay back four times more than he'd taken from anybody he'd ever cheated.

It wasn't too late for Zacchaeus, because Jesus is the God of the comeback.

See, we don't need to shine ourselves up and sit in a beautiful church sanctuary. We don't need to gather our children and spouse together and figure out how to become the world's most functional family. We don't need to get well *before* we meet Jesus. That's what he does for us!

It doesn't matter how messy life has become; it's never too late for God to do a miracle. It's never too late for God to restore your family, your health, your mind. It's never too late for him to put your life back together. It's never too late to heal the wounds inflicted on you over years. It's never too late for Jesus to speak to you when you're hanging on a cross in the middle of your guilt and the punishment you deserve. It's not too late if you're in a garbage dump and you don't matter to anyone in this world.

The good news is that paradise connects with landfills. Today, thanks to Jesus, paradise can come to us.

That's what Jesus is like. Jesus is always a light in the darkness. He's not afraid to walk into any situation at any moment. Anyone in any condition can say, "Jesus, will you remember me? I need you. I need a savior. I need a comeback." To them, Jesus always says, "Yes, I will be the connection between you and paradise."

Your fresh start begins today.

Caution: Don't dismiss the idea of a comeback if you're

someone who is already saved and walking faithfully with the Lord. You may need a fresh start after you find that your dreams—holy dreams—have crashed into pieces at your feet. Ever been in those circumstances?

THREE

WHEN DREAMS ARE DASHED

Twenty-three-year-old Jarryd Wallace can't remember a time when he wasn't competitively running. He was born with running in his blood. As a baby, he was pushed in a stroller the length of a full marathon even before he could walk. He grew up winning almost every race he ran, and he always did well as a runner in school. Everybody had high hopes for him. The word *Olympics* was even whispered as a big dream that could be within reach someday.

Going into his senior year of high school, he signed with the University of Georgia to run for them on an athletic scholarship, despite having been diagnosed with chronic exertional compartment syndrome—an exercise-induced muscle and nerve condition that causes pain and swelling—earlier that year.

He'd felt those symptoms for a while, about four years actually. At first the problems hadn't seemed serious—just too much pressure in his calves. But the pain wouldn't go away, no matter what he tried. And the pain kept growing worse.

Finally Jarryd had surgery to correct the problem, but complications set in. Serious complications. He lost about 60 percent of the muscle in one leg from his knee down. But he was determined to run, no matter what. One day he tried to run around the track, but the pain was too great. He completed the lap, crossed the finish line, and fell on his face in tears, anger, and desperation before God. Jarryd knew his dream was over. At that low point, however, he decided to keep on running— only now he was going to run away from God. Over the next few months he started drinking, doing drugs, and sleeping around. Nothing could quench the pain he felt in his heart.

The physical complications with his leg only grew worse. One day Jarryd heard the words that changed his life forever. His disease-wracked leg needed to be amputated. There was no other way forward.

When he was twenty years old, Jarryd had his leg removed. The surgery was successful. Six weeks to the day after that amputation, Jarryd walked pain-free for the first time in four years—using a prosthetic leg. Twelve weeks after the amputation, he ran again.

Jarryd set a new goal: to run in the Paralympic Games. And not only run but set a world record. He started training, but bursitis set in. One day Jarryd was resting on the couch at home, and God used that quiet, small moment to impress upon his heart that he still had a hope and a future for Jarryd. God seemed to be saying, *It doesn't matter if you do important things. What matters is that you draw close to me.* Jarryd started heading back to God. In time the bursitis went away, and Jarryd resumed training.

Jarryd qualified for the US team that was heading to London in 2012. He qualified in two events: the 400-meter sprint and the 4 x 100 relay. He and his teammates had high expectations to run well. But the time going in to the big event was nerve-racking, and everyone on the team ended up having a horrible day. Jarryd tripped on one of his exchanges during the relay and nearly fell.

The team finished third in the race, only to find out later that they'd been disqualified because one of the runners had stepped over the line during an exchange.

Jarryd was devastated. That night, sitting frustrated in his room, he asked God what was the purpose behind all his trials. God seemed to say: *I've given you an amazing story. When you go back home, I want you to share this story. More people will be able to relate to a stumble than they will a medal.*

So Jarryd shared his story. And he kept running. The next year, for the world championships in France, Jarryd qualified for the 100 meter, 200 meter, and the 4 x 100 relay. During the prelims of the 200, Jarryd gave it his all and he broke the world record.

There were a lot of interviews afterward that Jarryd didn't feel prepared for. One question that kept coming up was, "Are you going to go faster tomorrow?" All he could say was an honest "I hope so."

That night he thought about those interviews, and he remembered how unsatisfied the interviewers had been. For Jarryd, all of the questions were an echo of the world telling him his best is never going to be good enough. Yet Jarryd felt that the Lord, by contrast, was satisfied with him, because he had found his satisfaction in God. *The race has already been won*, God impressed on his heart. *All I'm asking you to do is show up and let my light shine through you.*

The next day Jarryd ran free. He crossed the finish line and set a new world record in the 200 meter. Amazingly, he had beat his own world record!

Today, on the blade that now serves as his lower leg, Jared has inscribed one short phrase that tells it all: IRun4Him.

You might not have lost a limb, but I bet you've lost something of value. Chances are good that you once had a dream—a big, noble, beautiful dream—that you could envision coming true, but that dream was snatched away. An experience like that leaves you longing for a comeback.

Sometimes we blow it, make terrible choices, and need to come back from our own sin, failure, and mistakes. There was a dream in your heart, and you believed your life would unfold according to that dream. Yet your decisions knocked that dream off the rails. Everything went haywire, and the dream you felt was from God collapsed. What then?

Or, circumstances beyond your control shut down the hope you were carrying for your future. What next?

All of us can relate to those experiences. If you're going through something similar right now, know that God still has a plan to use your life in a significant way. That thought may be just a seed in your heart for now, but it can grow into a great truth. I don't know exactly what you've lost, but I know this for sure: God isn't finished with you yet.

Jesus is a dream restorer. Your life might look different now than when it was born in your heart, but heaven still has a plan for you. Our invitation is to write on our circumstances the same thing Jarryd wrote on his blade.

I run for him.

A Youthful Dream

Genesis 37–50 tells the story of a teenager named Joseph who had a dream from God. Maybe as a teenager you pictured your future or you felt a calling to pursue a certain direction, and you were convinced life would unfold a certain way. Then somehow the dream evaporated in a moment or over a series of events that you didn't see coming.

Joseph was a direct descendant of the patriarch Abraham through Abraham's son Isaac and then through Isaac's son Jacob. Joseph, one of the twelve sons of Jacob, was his dad's favorite. The Bible tells us Jacob made Joseph a coat of many colors. This didn't help Joseph's reputation among his brothers, who already resented him as their dad's pet. How does something like that go down today? Maybe your parents favored your brother or sister or maybe *you* were the favorite. You've always known it, it feels good, and you want to text your siblings right now to remind them. But favoritism can be rough stuff.

Joseph had a crazy dream in which his brothers all bowed down to him. Here's a hint for successful living: if you ever have a dream where your brothers bow down to you, don't tell your brothers about the dream. Joseph made the mistake of sharing. "By the way," he said, "I've had a dream from God, and here's how it's going to go for all of you guys: you're all going to bow down to me." And the brothers said, "Yeah, right. I don't think so, kid."

One day the brothers were tending their father's flock in Dothan, and Jacob sent Joseph to check on them. The brothers, fed up with all the favoritism and what they took as Joseph's bragging, saw him coming and were filled with hatred. They decided to take him out. Since they were away from home, they could concoct a story for their dad and he'd never know the difference. Along came the dreamer, and the brothers grabbed him and threw him down an abandoned dried-up well, a pit probably ten to fifteen feet deep. The brothers discussed killing him, but some suggested another plan.

Just then a caravan came across the horizon. One brother said to the others, "Let's sell Joseph to the gypsies but tell Dad we found his coat on the roadside. Dad will assume some terrible fate came to him."

The rest of the brothers thought this sounded like a good plan. So at age seventeen, Joseph was sold into slavery. The brothers took his fancy coat, ripped it to shreds, smeared an animal's blood on it, and lied through their teeth to their dad when they got back home. "Nope, we didn't see any sign of him, but we found this tattered coat."

Jacob gasped and wept. The brothers stood there, tight-lipped, with the money jingling in their pockets while their dad sobbed with grief.

As the story unfolds, the traders took Joseph to Egypt's slave market to make a profit on the deal. He was put on the auction block and sold to Potiphar, a leader under Pharaoh.

Potiphar was the captain of the guard—an important person. With him begins a silver lining in the midst of this story. Joseph, this seventeen-year-old kid fresh from the backside of nowhere, was trained in the ways of running Potiphar's house for a while. Scripture says, "The LORD was with Joseph . . . in the house of his Egyptian master" (Genesis 39:2).

And Joseph did well—even as a household slave. He rose up through the ranks. Potiphar recognized Joseph's potential, made him head over domestic affairs, and gave him the run of the house. Even in slavery things seemed to be going as well as they could, under the circumstances.

But Potiphar's wife was scheming to get her hands on Joseph.

One day while Potiphar was away on business, she lured Joseph into her bedroom and made a move toward him. Joseph could have had Potiphar's wife in that moment, but he resisted. He told her, "Your husband has put me in charge of his entire household, but obviously you belong exclusively to him. He has trusted me and I want to honor him and honor myself and honor God." Joseph backed away in a hurry and ran.

Potiphar's wife was beside herself with frustration. As Joseph ran, she grabbed his garment and ripped off part of his robe. In a flash she concocted a devilish story and started chasing after him, yelling to the servants, "He tried to take advantage of me!"

Potiphar's wife felt scorned, she was fuming mad, and she twisted the facts in a big way.

When Potiphar came home, she accused Joseph again. Potiphar probably knew how it really went down, knowing his wife and knowing Joseph, and he connected the dots. Instead of executing Joseph on the spot, which he'd have done if Joseph had really been guilty as charged, he threw Joseph in prison.

How's that for a résumé? Dreamer, slave, prisoner. Things seemed to be progressing from bad to worse for Joseph. After all the commotion died down, Joseph heard the gates clang shut and found himself on a dungeon floor, his dreams up in smoke.

Dungeon Dreams

Have you ever had a dream evaporate right before your eyes?

Maybe Joseph had been thinking that things had been looking up, even though his brothers had mistreated him. Now he was in prison and his dreams looked completely hopeless again.

Where could he go from there? A month passed and then another and then another. This was not a judicial system that guaranteed a speedy trial.

Joseph wasn't alone in the slammer. Time passed, and two men joined Joseph in prison: Pharaoh's former cupbearer and Pharaoh's former baker. Both of these guys had dreams they didn't know what to do with, and their dreams troubled them. They got to talking one day, the three of them, and Joseph said, "Hey, I'm good with dreams—with God's help. I'll try to help you." So the two men told him their dreams.

Joseph interpreted for the cupbearer, saying, "Good news, your dream is going to have a good ending."

But to the baker he said, "Not so good for you." We don't know exactly how their conversation went. Maybe Joseph first said to the baker, "You don't want to know what your dream means," and maybe the baker insisted. "Nah, tell me, I can take it." Whatever happened, Joseph told him that his head would be cut off and stuck on a pole and birds would peck his eyes out. Talk about a nightmare.

And that's exactly what happened. The baker lost his life, but the cupbearer was restored to his position. Joseph asked the cupbearer to put in a good word for him, and the cupbearer nodded and said he would. But he "did not remember Joseph, but forgot him" (Genesis 40:23). Time passed and then more time passed and still more time passed. Eventually two years went by. Every day down at the jail, Joseph expected the jailer to bring him a message, but Joseph was forgotten—until Pharaoh himself had a dream.

Take note: God is a dream-giving God. He's given you and me dreams.

As the true leader of his nation, God put a dream in Pharaoh's mind. But no one could interpret the dream for Pharaoh. One day the cupbearer heard about it, and something clicked in his memory. *Oh yeah, there was this guy—what was his name?—down at the jail. He was good with my dreams.* The cupbearer told Pharaoh, "Sir, if you need help with a dream, I know someone who can help."

So Joseph was summoned into Pharaoh's presence. This was no small matter. Joseph washed and scrubbed, shaved, and changed into his best clothes. Pharaoh told him the dream, and Joseph, giving credit to God, told him the meaning: "Egypt will have seven amazing years of bumper crops and seven years of banner financial reports. But they will be followed by seven years of the worst famine you've ever seen. God gave the dream to prepare you."

Pharaoh was a man of action. He knew Joseph had interpreted the dream correctly. Immediately, impressed with the Hebrew's wisdom and discernment, he put Joseph in charge of preparing for the coming famine. On that day Joseph went from prisoner to second-in-command of all of Egypt. His task: guide the nation through the seven years of plenty and be ready for the lean years to come.

Sure enough, the famine came. It affected not only Egypt but even Canaan, where Joseph's family still tended sheep. The famine hit hard, and his family's farms dried up, crops failed, animals died, and the family faced starvation.

They heard the rumor about food in Egypt, so Joseph's brothers traveled to Egypt to buy grain. Guess who they met? They didn't recognize the man in charge as their brother Joseph. It had been years since they last saw him at the bottom of the pit.

The man they encountered now was wearing all the trappings of regal rule.

But Joseph recognized them, and he recognized the plan of God unfolding in front of his eyes.

Where Are We in Joseph's Story?

How do we relate to a guy way back in time, a guy like Joseph? He was thrown into a pit, sold into slavery, betrayed, imprisoned, forgotten. But his story is closer to our stories than we may think at first glance.

Have you ever been abandoned? Left behind? Sold out? Maybe not dropped literally down a dry hole, but that's how you felt.

Ever had your hopes run dry? Maybe the money ran dry, your heart ran dry, or you went through a whole season of dryness.

Have you ever been stabbed in the back? Maybe due a promotion, but somebody undercut you? Somebody told lies about you?

Maybe you had just gotten things going in the right direction, and then your life took a sudden downward spiral. It's amazing that Joseph went through all this and yet had the perspective to understand that God was at work the whole time.

That's the bigger story of Joseph. Even after he'd begun to do well a second time, it was all pulled out from under him again. Can you relate to feeling like everybody else is getting ahead and you're falling further behind? Others get recognized, but you seem to be invisible, and life moves on without you? That's exactly where Joseph was, but he never lost sight of God's work in his life.

How did Joseph manage to stay hopeful through it all?

There are at least five principles from Joseph's experience that we can inject into our circumstances when our dreams crumble. Try to adopt these five perspectives you feel like you're at the back of the line.

1. Your Story Is Part of God's Story

Joseph understood that the overall purpose of his life was to fit into a small part of God's larger plan for the world. Joseph understood that his life's purpose was bigger than simply playing out his own dream, even a God-given dream. He knew he was on earth to be part of God's story. This was a game changer for Joseph, and it can be a game changer for us too.

Maybe your dream is to go to school or get a degree or accomplish a certain task or find a spouse or start a business or move to a certain place or create a movement or carry the gospel to people who've never heard it before. Those may be great dreams, but there's a bigger dream that overrides everything else: it's that your life counts for the glory of God. That's the overriding dream of God's heart. If we don't embrace that dream, then we are in trouble, because all our smaller dreams are subject to change. That overarching dream never needs to change, and Joseph understood that.

Look at Genesis 42–45, one of the most powerful stories in the Bible. Joseph wanted his brothers to bring the whole family to Egypt, where they'd be safe from the famine, so he played a trick on his brothers. They didn't know what was going on, but he wanted to see if their hearts had changed. He wanted to see if they had learned to think about others instead of just themselves.

The brothers passed the test, and eventually Joseph revealed to them who he was. Finally he was reunited with his dad.

(Speaking of Jacob, Joseph's father, talk about a comeback. He probably still had the tattered coat from thirteen years ago, but now he sees his son alive. What a reunion and comeback!)

Finally, with all the family safely in Egypt and provided for, the brothers started thinking, *As long as Dad's alive, we're good, because he's our buffer. But Dad's getting old, and when he's gone, we're in trouble.* And when Jacob died, the brothers panicked (Genesis 50:15–18). They said to each other, "What if Joseph holds a grudge against us and pays us back for all the wrongs we did to him?" Just to be on the safe side, they sent word to Joseph: "Your father gave this command before he died. 'Say to Joseph, "Please forgive the transgression of your brothers and their sin, because they did evil to you."' And now, please forgive the transgression of the servants of the God of your father" (Genesis 50:16–17).

Anybody in today's world ever pull that on a brother or sister? Mom or dad passed away and you said, "By the way, the last thing Mom said was that I'm to get the house and you're not." Ugly stuff. These guys decided to pretend their dad had said this about forgiveness, and they hoped Joseph would go along.

"Joseph wept when they spoke to him" (v. 17). I don't think he wept over their message; he wept because he loved his dad and for the ugliness of his brothers' fear.

Then his brothers "came and fell down before him and said, 'Behold, we are your servants'" (v. 18). Joseph could have let his thoughts stray an unhealthy way. He could have thought: *How interesting. I seem to remember a dream where you all bowed down. What's this? You're actually bowing down. Well, hello. I was right after all.*

But Joseph didn't dwell on that; he focused on a higher story. When they said, "We are your servants," Joseph didn't answer back, "Yeah, you're right; you are my slaves." Instead, he said, "Do not fear" (v. 19).

That's how confident Joseph was. He asked, "Am I in the place of God?" Then he asked if the brothers were seeing what he was seeing in the situation—that God was behind it. He told them they didn't need to fear his position or power or comeback, because God had put him in this place. Joseph said to them, "'You meant evil against me, but God meant it for good, to bring it about that many people should be kept alive, as they are today. So do not fear; I will provide for you and your little ones.' Thus he comforted them and spoke kindly to them" (vv. 20–21).

I don't know if more powerful words were ever spoken by a human. We know that the God-man, Jesus, said amazing things. But Joseph was a human, like you and me, and yet he was so in touch with God's sovereignty. How do you come to understand that what people intended for evil, God intended for good? Joseph was saying that the sovereign God was over all the affairs of the world. Brothers are not in charge. Circumstances are not in charge. God is in charge. Joseph never lost sight of God's love and purpose, and he knew God was using him to bring glory to himself and salvation for many people.

This is a powerful, powerful, powerful way to live. Sure, this mind-set doesn't preclude doing our best to right wrongs, seek justice, and find cures. But in the process of taking action, we must understand that God is in charge.

We need to fight a battle to see this truth. When bad things happen, the Enemy comes through the door and tells us that God doesn't love us anymore and has no plan for us, and then we tend to bail out on God. But Joseph tells us, "Don't abandon God, because even in the pit, God has a plan. Even when you feel abandoned, God is still on the scene. Even when you can't see what God is doing, he's always doing something."

Through the lens of God's grace, we can look back on the thirteen lost years of Joseph's life and see that these were actually saving years, not only for Joseph, but for his entire family and many others. If we can grasp that one idea, it frees us from feeling we are in charge of any circumstances. We are released to trust our lives into the hands of a loving God.

In the previous chapter we looked at the thief on the cross and his comeback story. With his last breath, the thief called out for mercy, and Jesus gave that mercy. Luke 23 tells us that darkness covered the earth while Jesus hanged on the cross. The last thing Luke records about what Jesus says is, "'Father, into your hands I commit my spirit!' And having said this he breathed his last" (23:46). Nothing ever looked more wrong than the Son of the living God hanging on a cross, but Jesus knew about the bigger plan, and he trusted God with that plan.

Jesus said, "This is it for me, this is my last breath. I'll soon be in a position—dead—where I can't do anything to change anything. If there's going to be a resurrection, then I need to trust the Father for it." So into the Father's hands Jesus committed his spirit.

Joseph had that same attitude, and that's victory. Whatever circumstances we're in, they can't change the fact that, if we're willing, our lives are safely in God's hands. God takes responsibility to use us for his glory.

We may get into places where we're convinced God can't use our circumstances, or we try to manipulate the situation or figure out how to change the dynamic, and all we can really do is put our lives in God's hands. And that's all he's asking us to do.

So the first perspective we can adopt from Joseph is to see that our story is part of God's story.

2. God Goes the Distance with You

God was with Joseph the whole way. Don't ever let the Enemy say that if God is really with you then your circumstances would be different.

When the situation seems to be eroding from under our feet, the Enemy always arrives with the same speech: "If God really loved you, he'd do *something different* for you. Your circumstances would be different. Your circumstances would be better right now."

No. God always loves you. God is always for you. God always has a plan. And even in situations such as Joseph's, God is always with you. God is with you in the pit. He's with you when you're sold to the traders. He's with you on the auction block. He's with you in Potiphar's house and while you're facing temptation in the bedroom. He's with you in jail. He's with you when the cupbearer forgets you, when you're back in Pharaoh's court, through years of plenty and years of lean, and when brothers return. He's with you the whole time. It changes your outlook to know that almighty God is in every circumstance with you.

A disservice is done by any brand of Christianity that promises there's always going to be a better road ahead or insists that your circumstances will change or claims everything is going to work out right and all your wildest dreams will come true every time. No, we live on a broken planet. We're in a fight for our lives in a dying world. And we follow a Savior who was crucified in the middle of it all.

Sometimes our circumstances don't add up to the dream we

have envisioned, but that never means God isn't with us. Look at Hebrews 13:5, just one of the places where God promises, "I will never leave you nor forsake you."

That truth alone—God never leaves us nor forsakes us—that's a game changer. That's a comeback.

3. Our Best for the Master

The third perspective to adopt from Joseph's story is that we must offer God our very best.

Let's never adopt the attitude that says, "I was stabbed in the back and I'm stuck in this situation and should have had better, so I'll just go through the motions." Joseph certainly could have taken that attitude. He could have done every role as a servant halfheartedly. He could have cut corners at every turn. Who would care? But Joseph knew that's not God's way.

God is with you even when you are overlooked or treated unfairly. So if he is with you, then you want to do your best. God is right beside you in the process, whatever you're going through. So you want to keep doing your very best wherever you are. There is still a plan unfolding, and somebody has their eyes on you to see how you'll respond to these circumstances. Actually, it's probably true that more people have eyes on you in the pit than were watching when you came down the road in a multicolored coat.

Do you find yourself in a crummy situation? Do your best for the sake of God's glory.

4. Comeback Isn't About Payback

The fourth perspective Joseph's story teaches us is to be gracious when the tide turns, because we know we are in the plan of God and not the plan of men.

Let's be honest, part of the appeal of Joseph's comeback story is that we would like to be in a similar story where we would be in position to get back at the brothers and stick it to them.

If you're looking for a comeback only so you can stick it to somebody who was unfair to you, then stop right there. A better idea would be to tell that person that God is in charge of your life and they are not and never have been. Tell them you believe God is in charge of the arc of your life and you're free of animosity toward them. You're not saying that all consequences disappear, but you're saying that you forgive them because you are in God's story.

When you get your comeback, it's a powerful thing to extend grace. Thinking of acting vengefully? Thinking of rubbing someone's nose in the dirt? God isn't like that and neither are you. Always take the high road.

Comeback isn't about payback.

5. It's a Salvation Story

The fifth perspective to adopt is to know that your struggle is actually about somebody else's salvation. Wow. When Joseph first identified himself to his brothers before their father died, he said, "Come close to me." And when they did, he said, "I am your brother, Joseph, whom you sold into Egypt" (Genesis 45:4).

As though they had forgotten who their brother Joseph was! As if they had rolled into Egypt not remembering! Notice what Joseph says next: "And now do not be distressed or angry with yourselves because you sold me here, for God sent me before you to preserve life" (v. 5).

Take hold of that little phrase: *to preserve life.* What kind of thinking was that? That's supernatural, I'm-in-a-bigger-God-story thinking. That's powerful. That kind of thinking says my job every day is to put my life in God's hands. God's job every day is to use my circumstances for his glory.

Joseph explained this perspective to his brothers: "For God sent me before you to preserve life. For the famine has been in the land these two years" (vv. 5–6). The brothers didn't know how the future was going to go down, so Joseph told them: "And there are yet five years in which there will be neither plowing nor harvest. And God sent me before you to preserve for you a remnant on earth, and to keep alive for you many survivors" (vv. 6–7).

Jesus himself was to be born from the lineage of these people, and if they died during a famine in Canaan, there would be no lineage to bring us a Savior. God was working a really big plan, and today we're part of that plan. When we see Joseph in heaven—it may be a long line to thank him—we'll say something like, "Thank you for being faithful in the pit and with the traders and in Potiphar's house and when falsely accused, and thank you for not falling and for being faithful in jail and with Pharaoh, and thanks for showing kindness in the comeback." We stand in God's grace today because of Jesus, and Jesus came through the line of Jacob's family.

When we suffer, it's always for somebody's saving—that issue is always hanging in the balance. It's not all about me; it's all about Jesus becoming known in this broken world. Just like Joseph, whatever our suffering, God is always positioning us for someone's salvation.

As we read this story, lightbulbs go on because so much about Joseph reminds us of Jesus. As Jesus hung on the cross, looking down at his crucifiers, he asked God to forgive them because they didn't know what they were doing. The night Jesus was arrested, he was thrown into a dungeon in the high priest's house and abandoned. Jesus was sold for thirty pieces of silver, stabbed in the back by one of his own disciples, Judas. Jesus was forgotten. He hung alone and took on the suffering of the world to bring salvation for many. God sent him ahead of us so God could bring a great deliverance and a great salvation.

Joseph teaches us that our struggle is always for someone's salvation. That doesn't mean we should say, "Bring me more struggle because more people will get salvation." None of us runs eagerly into that battle. But when the battle comes to us, we know God is working a great purpose.

Your Ultimate Dream: God's Glory

At one time Jarryd went to the University of Georgia with the intention of running fast. That dream didn't pan out exactly as he hoped. But today Jarryd is preaching to a whole lot of people, and many people are coming to know Jesus though his story.

I don't know what you've lost, and I don't know what place you're in right now, but I know this: God isn't finished with you yet. You may not run the exact race you thought you would be running, but God still has a race for you.

You can write on your circumstances what Jarryd wrote on his blade: *I run for you, Jesus.* Believe that God will still use your life for the big dream, his glory, and the salvation of people.

Here are God's words as recorded in Jeremiah 29:11:

> For I know the plans I have for you . . . plans for welfare and not for evil, to give you a future and a hope.

This is the God we are invited to serve: a God who gives dreams and sees those dreams through. God is the same yesterday, today, and forever. The same God who spoke those words to the Israelites about a future and a hope is speaking them to you today. God has not forgotten you. God has not forgotten the dreams he's placed in your heart.

As we'll see in the next chapter, it doesn't matter how far you've gone, what you've done, or where you've been. This same God always throws the door wide open and says, "Welcome home!"

FOUR

WELCOME HOME

There are few things more frustrating than being locked out of your house. I mean, it's your house, but you can't get inside! Has that ever happened to you?

Many people hide a key outdoors in case this happens, but even then, getting locked out can still happen. Maybe you used that key the last time you were locked out and didn't put it back. Or maybe a friend came when you were out of town, and you told the friend where to find the hidden key, and he forgot to put it back. Or maybe you usually keep the key under the mat or the planter or above the light or by the gate near the trash cans, but wherever it's usually kept, it's not there today, and you're locked out of your house.

It happened to me not so long ago. I'd just been on a trip with Brad, one of my teammates on staff at our church. For the better part of five years, we traveled together almost everywhere I went. As a result, we ended up in a lot of interesting places at various times of the day and night.

That night we arrived back at my house around 3 a.m. from an out-of-town speaking opportunity. Shockingly, I did not have my key (it's at this point people who know me well smile and laugh). Brad didn't have a key to my house either. At first I thought, *No problem. Shelley is in the house.* So we knocked on the door and rang the bell—nothing. Then I remembered that Shelley was a sound sleeper and it was going to take a lot to wake her. Ah, I then remembered to punch in the code to the garage door. The door went up, but that inside door was locked, too, and there was no spare key in the spot where it's supposed to be.

We walked around the house, checking windows and doors. I thought we might need to break a window. It didn't make any sense, but it made more sense than going to a nearby hotel, sleeping in the car, or driving all the way to Brad's house at 3 a.m.

Finally, we came around to the front door—the one door we hadn't checked—and had the bright idea to actually try it. It opened! Now, Shelley and I are usually very, very careful to lock our doors, but that night, for some strange reason, the front door wasn't locked. What a relief! I had no real problem after all, only a perceived problem.

I stepped inside—home at last!

Welcome or Exclusion?

That picture of being locked out is a picture of the frustration people sometimes feel when they approach the church. Sadly, the church as a whole has too often made people in our society feel locked out of the house where they really belong. They are locked out of a relationship with God.

As individual churches, sometimes we present an image that's high and mighty, and we build walls around the church or the faith that are so great that a lot of people who are falling short feel they can't get in. We even alter our language—words, phrases, tone—all changed just a bit from the way we normally speak. We create a subculture, and if you don't know the right words and inflections, the door code and the secret knock, then you're not going to get in.

That type of exclusion sends a horrible message: We are in and you are out. We've done it right and you've done it wrong. We've stayed on the straight and narrow, but you, my friend, are an idiot who has blown your life.

If that kind of rejection has been your experience, then I want you to know that Jesus actually sends a completely different message. Whatever you've done, wherever you've been in life, Jesus says that you need to hear this:

Welcome home!

Try the front door, because it's open. Come on in. You're always welcome in the house of God. It's not about gaining access to a church building, but rather that you are always welcome to a relationship of friendship with God.

If you've been a Christian for any amount of time, then maybe you read those words with reservations. Some believers find troubled feelings percolating in their hearts when they hear sinners welcomed without conditions. You're worried that this chapter is going to say that anybody can come back to God regardless of what they have done, no matter how ridiculous their disobedience has been, how far they've run away, or what they've shoved in the face of God or people. They get a free pass back to God, and that makes you uncomfortable.

Let's push past the discomfort and look closely at what the Bible says about this. Luke 15 opens by describing a scene. Let these words from Scripture sink into your mind and heart:

The tax collectors and sinners were all gathering around to hear Jesus. But the Pharisees and the teachers of the law muttered, "This man welcomes sinners and eats with them." (vv. 1–2 NIV)

What stands out here is the word *welcomes*. Welcome is supposed to be the hallmark of the church. *Welcome* means

- We don't build high walls.
- We don't put gates at the end of the road.
- We don't put obstacles in front of people.

Instead, we roll out a red carpet and a big welcome mat in front of people, and all of this says, "Are you looking for a place to belong? You've found it! Welcome home! Are you looking for God? He's here! Are you looking for grace? We have found it. Welcome home!"

Like Jesus, we are supposed to welcome those who are failing and flailing, and actually share the humble human act of eating with them. But there's tension in this scene that Luke tells us about too, because the system back then had become stilted. In that outwardly religious culture, a person's standing with God was based on an ability to prove that one stood above the average riffraff. There was a spiritual pecking order. You did this and didn't do that. You acted this way but not that way. And it all built status. You talked to these people but not those people, all the while waiting for the Messiah. (Yes, the religious types back then regularly checked the horizon, wondering if that guy coming down the road or the next guy was the Messiah, the Promised One.)

Then Jesus appeared on the scene. He made claims that sounded Messiah-like. Some people immediately wondered if this guy might be *the* guy, the Messiah. But Jesus perplexed the Pharisees, the most religious people of the day. They acknowledged that Jesus had power and did miracles and lots of people wanted to follow him. But he didn't fill the bill of the Messiah they were looking for because he hung out with sinners. They were scandalized by that. *Nobody who comes from God would do that*, they thought. *No one sent from heaven would welcome the worst people and share a meal with them. The Messiah would be straitlaced and have nothing to do with that sort. He'd be looking for us, the superspiritual and uberreligious guys, to share his meals with.* That was the dynamic going on here. Sinners were getting closer to Jesus, and religious people were backing away from him.

The people with spiritual facades generated an undercurrent of noise. Can't you just hear the muttering? How could they ever think they could talk behind their hands with Jesus nearby, as if he couldn't hear? A bat with sonar has nothing on Jesus. He hears even our thoughts and understands everything that is going on inside our hearts. But they muttered, "Who is this guy? Where did he come from?"

Detecting and somewhat annoyed by their murmurs, he looked right at them and said, "I want to tell you a story."

Bringing Home a Stray Sheep

That's how Jesus answered the religious folks. Telling them stories and parables.

The first story was about a shepherd who had a hundred sheep. One ran off and was lost in a thicket in the woods. The shepherd still had ninety-nine sheep, and in most situations that would be a pretty good economic picture. He could have shrugged and told himself, "Oh, well, 99 percent is just fine."

But this shepherd did a surprising thing—he left the ninety-nine and went after the one lost sheep. He found it, carried it on his shoulders, and came home singing and shouting. He called his friends and told them the story of his search, stressing, "I found my lost sheep. This little guy is safely back in the fold. Rejoice with me." He was willing to leave the ninety-nine in order to bring home the missing one.

The point of the story is simple. Let's take any gathering where there are supposed to be, say, 2,000 people. If 1 percent of the crowd doesn't show up, just 20 people, God would say to the other 1,980 in the room, "Hold on," and he would go after the lost ones. After he'd found them, he'd say to them, "I know I have a whole room full of people, but I want you in the story too. You see, I know your name, and you matter to me."

On the Hunt for a Missing Coin

Jesus then told them a second story about a woman who had ten coins and lost one of them. She didn't say, "Oh, I still have nine coins, and that's not bad." Ninety percent attendance at most church meetings would be stellar. We wouldn't worry much about the missing few. But she wasn't satisfied with 90 percent of her treasure.

The coin was probably part of a string of coins that formed her headpiece, signifying that she was a married woman. Losing part of this headpiece was like losing a stone from a wedding ring.

She searched for the missing coin. She turned the house upside down, turned the furniture over, and looked under everything. Then she looked again.

Yes, she found the coin, and then she called all her friends together and said, "Look at this! Rejoice with me!"

The lost coin was found!

Watching a Son Get Lost

Jesus had one more story for them, and this one took longer to tell.

A man had two sons, and the younger one came to him and demanded his half of the family money now. So the dad agreed, called his attorney and his financial planner, and split up the estate—half to the older son and half to the younger son. The papers were signed and stamped. Money was wired into the accounts of the sons, deeds transferred into their names. Actually, in that culture, the dad now owned nothing. But he was still living, so he was given a place of honor and respect, but all his wealth had gone to his sons.

Guess what the younger son did with his share? He gathered everything he had, set off for a distant country, and "squandered his wealth in wild living" (Luke 15:13 NIV).

That's a nice way to describe some pretty full-on partying. The younger son went out thinking he was in the money now, so he could go wherever he wanted and do whatever he wanted and live the kind of life that he thought would make him happy. So he squandered his wealth. One translation says, "He wasted his substance with riotous living" (KJV). We don't know exactly what kind of lurid tones this picture requires to be painted accurately. But at the end of what we would call a crazy weekend, the son found he had absolutely nothing left.

Now, if you've ever had one of those crazy weekends or a crazy time—however long—where everything blurs together in riotous, wild, unhealthy activities, then you know the feeling that hits you at the end of the ride. Maybe you've had a run like that at some point in your life. To fund your lifestyle, you went to an ATM and took out more than you should have, and then you went again and again until eventually the account was empty. You lived riotously for a while and blew it all. At the end, all you had left was empty bottles and cans, empty syringes and pill bottles, an empty heart, and an empty soul. Your heart felt like it went there, too, and most of your future with it.

I think this younger son felt a vacuum. Reading between the lines, we can see that he felt just like we do when we get ourselves into that kind of situation. Maybe we put our big bash on a credit card and go home and tell ourselves how awesome all that fun was and we'll worry about the cost later. Or maybe it was a lot heavier and longer term than that. Maybe we gambled ourselves into a deep hole or we had to beg, borrow, and steal to pay for our escapades.

Whatever happened, when it was all over and the party ended and the lights went out and he or she was gone, we were left feeling empty and fearful. We tell God we'll never do that again. But the undertow is strong and it sucks us back in. We beg God to get us out of this mess just one more time, and we promise that this is the last time. Desperate, we pray,

- Just get me out of this house alive and I'll never come back here.
- Just get me away from this computer and I'll never look at this stuff again.
- Just get this noose from around my neck and I'll never be involved with this situation again.

That's what happened to the younger son. At the end of the day, he didn't even have a single friend. He'd had a lot of friends before because he'd bought every round. Maybe he had something like a lake mansion, and people had flown over to party with him. But when the money runs out, it's amazing how fast the friends run out too. The son had not expected to find himself at this place in his journey—party over, money gone, no friends. "He had spent everything" (Luke 15:14).

Catch that word? *Everything!*

Have you ever spent everything?

Cleaned out your savings and your bank account? Borrowed from your roommate? Stolen from your parents? Spent it all? This son spent everything. Remember, his father's financial team had divided the estate between him and his brother, fair and square. The older brother likely had locked his share in a vault or invested it at 2.97 percent because that's the kind of hard-shell, conservative guy he was. But the younger brother spent every last dime.

Time passed, and a severe famine came to the whole country, and the younger brother was in serious need. He hired himself out to a farmer in that far country where he had gone, and he was sent to feed the pigs. The young man was so desperate that he even ate some of the pigs' food just to fill his empty stomach.

He had never planned on this. When he had started his spending spree, he didn't stop to consider that maybe he should put aside a little in case famine came. He didn't know famine was coming. We never know. But we can be assured that unexpected things are ahead whenever we walk away from God.

If this son had really been keeping in touch with his need, if he knew how much he was loved, he would have never left home. If he'd understood that he was truly home when he was home, he would not have left to look somewhere else for a place to belong.

But what clouds our view is the Enemy's skill at cropping photos. Everyone knows what it means to crop a picture, right?

In fact, it's likely some of you have cropped someone out of your social media profile pic. Maybe an old boyfriend or a roommate that was unnecessary. You liked the way you looked in that particular photo, so Jojo (or Janelle) had to go.

That's what happened on our honeymoon trip. The brochure promised a stunning Caribbean location and view. The half-moon beach was pristine, the green lawn a stark and vivid contrast. The water was like nothing I had ever seen; the palm tree-lined pool was breathtaking. I determined that would be our view and booked our stay for five days and four nights.

When we arrived I couldn't wait to get to the room, step out on the balcony, and check out our gorgeous brochure view. But as I flung open the balcony doors from our third-floor room, I was appalled to discover the half-moon beach in the photo was only *half the beach!* Much to my dismay, the other half of our idyllic, crescent bay was a hillside stacked with hundreds of abandoned, junked-out boats. Every kind of boat you can think of. Storm-damaged, rusted-out, broken-down boats piled on top of each other.

I shot back down to the front desk and asked for another room, but every room in the hotel faced the same direction and had the same troubled view. Frustrated, I pulled out the brochure (yes, I brought it with me) and said to the nice young lady working the desk, "Somebody cropped the boat graveyard out of my honeymoon!"

But isn't that just how the Enemy works? He causes us to lose sight of the good that's right in front of us and takes us down a road of imagination where we dream of a faraway land filled with everything our heart desires. The problem is he always crops the disaster out of our escape plans. Like the younger son, he masks the pitfalls and probable outcomes while highlighting the sizzle of the pleasure we're going to experience. Eventually, we discover the other side of the beach, the heartache that was really there waiting for us all along.

Returning from the Depths

It didn't take long for disaster to come into view, and for the wayward son to finally know he had hit rock bottom.

When he came to his senses, he said, "How many of my father's hired servants have more than enough bread, but I perish here with hunger! I will arise and go to my father, and I will say to him, 'Father, I have sinned against heaven and against you. I am no longer worthy to be called your son. Treat me as one of your hired servants.' And he arose and came to his father" (Luke 15: 17–20).

I love that last line: "He arose and came to his father." Now that's a comeback! The lost sheep didn't really need a dramatic comeback because it had just wandered off and didn't know which way was home. The shepherd had to find him and carry him back to the flock.

A lot of people don't know they are lost; they've just kind of wandered off. They don't know how they ended up in a thicket. They find themselves in a situation, a culture, or a flow of events, but they don't really know how they got there. They find themselves in a club or in our neighborhood or living in our condo with somebody that's caustic to them, and they don't know why they're in a particular geographic spot or why they're in a particular spiritual state. They just went with the flow. They don't really know they are lost. A lecture isn't in order. They just need someone to point them to a shepherd who says, "There's a home for you here. There's a place with grace, there's a God, and he has a family, and you are supposed to be in it." This person didn't know he was lost, but he's certainly happy to be found.

Think about the woman with the lost coin. What is she going to say to it? "Bad, bad coin!" No, she's going to look after her coins better in the future. There are some people who are lost in our neighborhoods because we, as God's family, are not looking after them well enough.

But the younger son was lost purposely. For him it was very deliberate. He intentionally wandered off. For some people the comeback story happens and they say, "Thank you, God, for coming and finding me. I didn't even know I was lost, much less how to get home." Other people's comeback stories are simply about being left behind by their spiritual family and then gathered in again, and they say, "Thank you, guys, for coming back for me. Thank you for searching and finding me."

But for some of us, our comeback story is like the younger son's. He made the move away from his father. He took the initiative to defy God. His actions were deliberate.

When we find ourselves in a similar place, our first step toward a comeback is to stand up in the mess and turn our hearts toward home.

For him and for us, it's not like God doesn't know where we are. This father lived in a country where news traveled fast and folks knew what was happening in the neighborhood. Rumor had come back to the father that the younger son's money was gone and the party was over. The father could have gone at any time to fetch him, but he knew that his son had to come to the end on his own. When the son hit bottom, he thought he would never be a son again. He approached his father with the thought that maybe he could live as a hired servant.

That's where the story takes a grace-ladened turn.

While he was still a long way off, his father saw him and felt compassion, and ran and embraced him and kissed him. (v. 20)

When the son started to come near, his father didn't miss it. It's clear from the story the father was eagerly waiting and just needed to see the top of his son's head over the horizon. He pulled his robe up, and this noble father started sprinting down the road, past the servants, past the gate, into the street toward his son.

The son must have thought the worst. First it was, *Who's the old man running down the road?* Then it was, *Oh no, that's my father. He's so angry he doesn't want to wait for me to get to the house to crush me; he wants to crush me right in full view of the street.*

But that's not how it went down. Before the son could even start his much-rehearsed speech, the father cried out, "This is my son," and threw his arms around him. Talk about a body slam, a chest bump, an amazing moment! This was no cordial hello—not a reserved, "Hi, son. Nice to see you again." We're talking about unchecked passion.

The son was dumbfounded.

The servants followed, and the father said, "What are you looking at? Get a robe! Put it on my son. Get a ring! Put it on his finger. Get shoes for his feet! Clean him up! Make him ready and—you over there—call Parties 'R' Us. Get everything ready. Kill the fatted calf and get that thing roasting. Call a band and the caterers. Start decorating, because we are having a party at our house tonight. My son was dead and he is alive again. He was lost and he is found, and we are going to celebrate!"

That's God.

That's God right there for us. If we "draw near to God . . . he will draw near to [us]" (James 4:8). And God doesn't hold back either. God doesn't hide around a corner or give a lecture or treat us like some kind of second-class worker. He just waits to see us on the horizon. When he sees us coming toward him, he runs down the road with his arms open wide.

But the older brother wasn't so forgiving. He came home from work at the end of the day. He heard the music and dancing and called a servant and asked what all the commotion was about. He was told that his brother had come home.

"I figured as much," the brother muttered. "I heard things went bust and figured he'd be crawling back here any day. But what's with the music and dancing?"

"That's just it," the servant offered. "Your dad has flipped out and is throwing a party for your brother!"

The older brother blew up at the thought of such kindness and extravagant, unmerited generosity and declared he wasn't going in. He apparently had some of that tension we talked about earlier—that says grace shouldn't be spread around so freely and people like this shouldn't be welcomed home so joyously.

Then the dad came out to talk to the older son. We don't know all that was said between them. What we do know is that the party went on and the younger son came back to life that night. Yep, the father (the picture of God in this story) threw a party and put on a dance for his son. What dance were they doing, you ask? They were doing the *comeback*!

Have you ever danced the comeback? The comeback is a crazy animated dance led by an always-good Father who grabs you onto the dance floor and says, "Let's dance." Even though you're now wearing a new robe and shoes and a ring, you're still thinking that everybody's looking at you like you're dirt. But the father comes and says, "I would like to start the first dance with my younger son. Come on, son. We're going to do the comeback." They move out on the dance floor, and the son is compelled by his father's great love. They dance because the father is the God of the comeback.

Think about it: each son received half the money, but one blew everything while the other shoved all his cash in a hole and kept working like he still needed to earn it.

God shows us in this story that both kinds of sons can have everything that belongs to the Father. If you put your faith in Jesus, you've got it. Yes, keep on working and help God bring the world to Jesus, but don't do it like you're poor or like you have to earn the Father's favor. Do it like you've received the wealth already. And you over there, you've got the wealth, too, so don't go living crazy. You've already got the best God can give.

But what do we do with the tension in this story? Aren't there consequences to people's foolish choices? Shouldn't somebody pay? For our answer, it helps to remember there is someone else in this story, and that's the one who is telling it. These stories are crossing the lips of Jesus, God in human flesh come to pay the price for our freedom. No one is getting off scot-free. Jesus is taking the blows for our wrongs, satisfying the wrath of a perfect God, and paving the way for us to be completely new in his love.

Sure, the younger son always lived with the fallout of his decisions. But right beside him the whole way was a Father whose compassion and forgiveness gave him strength to walk in confidence and humility into a brand-new future.

I want to tell you one more story, this one of a young man at our church. Dana is a living, breathing, walking miracle of the God of the comeback.

A Christmas Comeback

Dana grew up in an awesome home with amazing parents who loved him unconditionally. They gave him a great foundation, but in spite of all that, Dana ran from God and got into all the wrong stuff. In middle school, it was vandalism, fighting, and stealing. In high school, it was drugs and alcohol. By the time Dana left high school, he'd been arrested four times and was a suspect in several other crimes.

Dana went to military school to learn discipline, but he found himself right back in the same traps. He was drinking every night, doing drugs all the time. He was kicked out of school organizations and ultimately failed out of school. He couldn't keep a job. He overdosed on cocaine. He overdosed on heroin. He spent most of his late teenage years and his twenties in and out of jail and on probation. He got to the place where despair overwhelmed him, and he had no hope for the future. His was a story where he'd once had so much, but he'd squandered it all. Something desperately needed to change.

During the 2009 Christmas season, Dana was at the bottom of the bottom. He partied through the holidays in some of the worst hotels, doing some of the worst things imaginable. It was a Christmas without hope.

He'd been familiar with Jesus when he was a boy, and something changed that Christmas when the dust settled. Dana just knew that it was time to go back. On December 29, 2009, while having lunch with a pastor, Dana decided to give his life to Christ. Dana laid down alcohol, cigarettes, drugs, everything—he did it all at once. He got saved and sober, and his life since then has been on fire for Christ.

Jesus put the pieces of Dana's life back together. Jesus restored all of the relationships that needed to be restored. Dana and his parents spend time together these days and have a really strong relationship. When he looks back now, Dana knows that Jesus never, ever let go of him.

You can tell from Dana's story that he found out that no matter how far you've run or how long you've been running, the door of Jesus' house is always open and there's a welcome mat. You can find this out too. Yes, Jesus welcomes sinners. You think that sounds too easy? *Easy* isn't the right word for this welcome. Remember, they killed a fatted calf for that party in the story, but they killed Jesus himself, the storyteller, for the party God wants to throw for you. The price has been paid in full and forgiveness is on the table today. All you have to say is, "I want to come back home." The Father is waiting to throw his arms around you. That's the kind of comeback we're talking about.

That kind of comeback is available to you.

But be careful. Just when you're dancing with the Father on the great dance floor, that is when Satan tries to cut in and tell you it was all a dream. The Father doesn't really love you after all. He was just kidding when he ran down the road to greet you.

That's a lie. If you're still breathing, it's not too late.

FIVE

NEVER TOO LATE

So far we've seen how comeback stories may be about underdogs who triumph or about top dogs who crash but return to the top.

We've looked at how we all need that deeper comeback of the soul.

We've learned there are different kinds of comebacks. Some people come back from sin and waywardness, some from mistakes and failure, and others from dashed dreams.

We've looked at how we all need to come back home to God, that we're welcome there whether we've wandered or intentionally rebelled. Every comeback story is a human story intersecting with God's story. Everybody in this drama that God is writing can have a comeback story.

But maybe you're thinking that the comeback principle is all well and good *for other people*. For you, it's simply too late. The Enemy has deposited a boatload of hopelessness into your world. You might think you've gone too far, you've stepped over the line of no return, you've blown all your chances, it's over.

Maybe you think it's too late for any kind of comeback because you're too jaded or too scarred or maybe you think you're simply too old. Life feels like it's running out too fast, and there isn't enough time left to turn around in any significant way.

The legendary singer Johnny Cash was known as the Man in Black, but in a lot of senses he could be called the king of comebacks. He spent much of his life coming back from his addictions and problems that tore through his family like tornadoes. Cash's comebacks were genuine turnarounds, but then he would slip back into a lifestyle that as a child of God he had deplored. He had career comebacks, too, returning from near oblivion to the top of the charts in the country, rock, and gospel music worlds.

Possibly his biggest comeback came near the end of his life. Johnny was nearly blind by then, suffering with advanced diabetes. He could no longer walk and was under constant nursing care. He had suffered the loss of his pillar of strength, his beloved wife, June Carter Cash. In the car on the way home from her funeral, Johnny turned to his son and said, "I have to get to work. I have to get into the studio."[1]

Four days later, they were in the studio, recording, laying down track after track. "Such resolve could only have come from God," said John Carter Cash. "The place where he found the greatest solace was in the studio."[2] In a burst of strength, Johnny recorded sixty more songs in the few months he had left. He presented a surprise public concert, singing, among other songs, the iconic "Ring of Fire." It was a comeback that was a tribute to his wife and his God. Johnny Cash died September 12, 2003, just a little more than three months after his wife June. Johnny stepped out of his personal ring of fire and into the arms of his Father, the last comeback he'd ever need.

Whatever you need to come back from, I want you to hear

---

1 John Carter Cash, *Anchored in Love: An Intimate Portrait of June Carter Cash* (Nashville: Thomas Nelson, 2007), 187.

2 Ibid., 189.

this: if Jesus is alive from the dead—and he is—and if Jesus has conquered death and hell—and he has—then it's possible for every person to have a comeback story.

It's never too late.

You're not too far gone.

You're not too old.

You're not too far away.

When It Looks Like It's Too Late

Samson had every reason to feel like it was too late for him. He had blown it badly, repeatedly, wholly, and it looked as if time had run out for him. His is a tragic story of a series of collisions, mostly of his own making, but it has a redemptive ending.

Samson's story is found in the book of Judges and happens during a time we can easily relate to. The nation of Israel was in trouble, and if you've read the Bible much, then you know Israel was usually in trouble. They had a cycle, told especially in Judges, where God would work powerfully to cause things to go well for them, but as soon as they had been blessed, they would forget God, return to their own ways, and end up in trouble all over again. Sometimes God would purposely let them become subject to another nation, and this would shake them to the bottom of their soul. They'd admit, "God, we really messed up again. We need your help." Once again God would pour out his mercy and restore the nation. And then Israel would repeat the cycle time after time.

These are our spiritual ancestors, and they form a long line of people who, down through the centuries, as soon as things started to go smoothly, rebelled against God and ended up in predicament after predicament. Just as he did with Israel, God may let us slide under the rule of circumstances that we don't like. He allows it so the situation can squeeze us, so we can get over ourselves and get to the bottom. Because it's at the bottom where we turn to God and admit we've messed up and ask for his mercy and restoration. A lot of us need a shakedown so we can rise up. That's where Israel was at this time.

The Bible lays out the situation plainly: "Again the Israelites did evil in the eyes of the LORD" (Judges 13:1 NIV). Because of that evil, the Lord delivered them into the hands of the Philistines for forty years. There wasn't anything worse for an Israelite. It would be similar to being a Georgia Bulldogs fan, and after you messed up your life, you were compelled to cheer for the Florida Gators for forty years. You even have to live in Gainesville, wear an alligator costume, go to The Swamp every weekend, and do the gator chomp—for forty years.

That may be a silly illustration, but for Israel, this was serious oppression. They'd clashed with the Philistines before and would again many times. The boy, David, once took food to his brothers on the front lines of fighting against the Philistines. The problem was that the Philistines had LeBron James on their team. Well, they had the Old Testament version of the biggest guy anybody had ever seen. His name was Goliath, and he was so formidable that all the soldiers of Israel shook in their armor whenever he was around. Goliath taunted them and their God. But David came on the scene and said, "I believe God is bigger than that guy." David had learned a lot about God out under the stars while he was looking after the family's sheep, playing his harp. Before Goliath knew what happened, a smooth stone struck him squarely between the eyes and he went down. The little shepherd boy then grabbed Goliath's sword and lopped off the giant's head. That day the army of Israel carried David around on their shoulders and routed the Philistines.

The Philistines were a long-term enemy, and as we pick up the story of Samson, we learn it's at a time when Israel had disobeyed God and was in the hands of their worst enemy.

Are you in that kind of place? Maybe you're in some really difficult place because of an act of foolishness. You can choose to curse the place you're in, or you can remember that it's your fault you're there. The way out is to admit, "It was me who got myself here," and you can take a direct route through the grace of Jesus back to God.

By repentance you can get back on track faster, but Israel stayed under Philistine rule for forty years. God didn't want that. He's a God of mercy, a rescuer, not mean and evil. He's a gracious God who wants to deliver his people. Will they let him?

Will *you* let him deliver you?

A Spark of Hope

The story of Samson begins with some background: "A certain man of Zorah, named Manoah, from the clan of the Danites, had a wife who was unable to give birth" (Judges 13:2 NIV).

We may wonder why these details are important. It's because God is setting up a comeback story for his people to restore and bless them. He's going to raise up a judge, a new leader, and Manoah and his wife are to be the parents of that judge.

The angel of the Lord told Manoah's wife she was going to

have a son. Manoah may have thought, *You have me mixed up with someone else, because my wife can't bear children, and this is not going to work.* But it does work. This is a small comeback story in itself, and it tells us that small comeback stories can trigger bigger comeback stories. In your case, your comeback is going to set in motion a comeback for somebody else. When you return to Jesus, God may open the door for a whole string of people to be delivered.

The story is never just about you and me; it's always about God's glory and his work on planet Earth. We need to grasp this: it's not all about me and my issues and my deliverance. It's about God's purposes in the world. He needs to get me involved in his plan because I'm connected to a bunch of other people and their involvement with his plan. There may be five million people waiting right now for you to get your heart right with Jesus. Who knows what kind of dominos will fall when you finally bow to him?

For Manoah and his wife, just having a baby was a powerful comeback. That was their miracle. But it was only the beginning. They named him Samson, and according to the Scripture, God was with him: "He grew and the LORD blessed him, and the Spirit of the LORD began to stir him" (Judges 13:24–25 NIV).

Samson was purposed by God to do something phenomenal for God's people, and he had two big things going for him:

- A huge calling on his life.
- An incredible power on his life.

Within that potential, Samson did some amazing things. He killed a lion with his bare hands. That's pretty cool. Another time he killed thirty men by himself. Remember, this was wartime, and he was supposed to do this. How many people do you know who can face thirty-to-one odds and come out the winner? Then the Philistines did something terrible to his family, so Samson caught three hundred foxes, tied their tails together in pairs with torches, and chased them through the Philistines' fields, burning their crops. It never says that the particular method was sanctioned by God, but it's amazing that Samson actually pulled it off. On another occasion he used a donkey's jawbone to strike down a thousand Philistines. So the Philistines dreaded Samson. He was Goliath to them, and *they* were shaking in *their* boots this time.

But there was something about Samson that would take him down time after time. In addition to his unusual power and calling from God, a huge internal battle raged within the man—a struggle with women. As a young man he told his parents he wanted to marry a Philistine girl, and against their good advice, he went ahead and did it. As Samson's story unfolds, we see a systemic pattern of temptation with women.

Outwardly, God's favor is on Samson and God still uses him—this is a mysterious thing. Internally, a hurricane is brewing. Both of these outward and inward scenes are happening in Samson's life at the same time.

"One day Samson went to Gaza, where he saw a prostitute. He went in to spend the night with her" (Judges 16:1 NIV). How far he had fallen in his struggle with sexual temptation! The people of Gaza found out Samson was there, so some surrounded the prostitute's house while others set up an ambush for him all night at the city gate. "They made no move during the night, saying, 'At dawn we'll kill him'" (v. 2 NIV). But Samson snuck out in the middle of the night. On his way, he grabbed the city gates with his bare hands and ripped them out with the two posts, bar and all. He hoisted them on his shoulders and carried them about forty miles to the top of a hill near Hebron. He seemed to be saying, "Don't mess with me, because I have an incredible power you know nothing about." God's power came through for him all right, but still, Samson didn't learn his lesson.

> Some time later, he fell in love with a woman in the Valley of Sorek whose name was Delilah. The rulers of the Philistines went to her and said, "See if you can lure him into showing you the secret of his great strength and how we can over-power him so we may tie him up and subdue him. Each one of us will give you eleven hundred shekels of silver." (Judges 16:4–5 NIV)

The Valley of Sorek was an in-between place, with Philistine land on one side and Israelite land on the other. It's a practical reminder to us that there are some places we don't have any business going. But here was Samson, and he saw this dangerous woman and fell in love with her. I don't think this was a one-off. Samson had been in trouble with women before, and it seems to have become the pattern of his life. When he saw Delilah, he said, "I've got to have that woman!" But here's the funny thing: Delilah's name comes from root words meaning "low" and "hanging." Basically, her name means "easy." The Enemy knew Samson had this internal struggle, and so the Enemy put low-hanging temptation where he couldn't miss it.

You may have noticed that the Enemy doesn't come right out and blurt, "Hey, I want to wreck your life." More likely he takes an indirect route and asks, "Have you ever tried this? It won't hurt. Just this once." He knows your particular struggles, and he is really good at putting low-hanging temptation right in your grasp.

Delilah appeared on the scene when Samson was in a place he shouldn't have been in the first place.

Be careful whom you fall in love with, because your better judgment can be overwhelmed by your emotions. You know when a situation isn't God's best, so don't just drift along and tell yourself, "I can always fix the problems later." Before you know it, emotion kicks in and there goes your judgment. All of a sudden, you are in a serious relationship with someone whom—if you thought about it honestly—you know you shouldn't be with.

Well, Samson was blindly in love with Delilah, and the Philistines plotted to take advantage of that. To Delilah, the shekels looked really good. She accepted the Philistine bribe and made a bold move. She came right out and asked Samson the secret of his strength. We may think that Samson's common sense would click in. He should have thought, *Wait a minute. Time-out. I'm in enemy territory, and you want to know the secret of my strength? Why would you ask that? Could this be a setup? I wonder if she's being paid off.*

But Samson played along and said, "If I were tied up with seven bowstrings, I'd be as weak as a kitten." When he went to sleep, and I guess he was a heavy sleeper, Delilah tied him up with seven bowstrings and then shouted, "Samson! Quick! The Philistines are coming!" He woke up, broke the bowstrings, and bolted for the door.

So Delilah said, "Samson, why did you do that to me, honey, sweetheart? Come on now, what's really your secret, baby?"

So he told her that a brand-new rope would hold him. He fell asleep again and she tied him up with a brand-new rope and yelled that the Philistines were coming. He woke up and snapped the rope. This was becoming a game. They were teasing each other back and forth. But it was a deadly game.

You'd think Samson would clue in about this. But again Delilah sweet-talked him. He told her, "Braid my hair into seven braids and weave them into the weaver's loom." And then he slept, and while he slept, she did the deed and woke him up by shouting that the Philistines were coming. Just as he had done previously, he awoke and broke his confinement. There goes one good loom. So she's just mad now. Can't you just hear her saying these next words?

"How can you say, 'I love you,' when you won't confide in me?" (v. 15 NIV).

How common is that? Ever heard of a couple in an unwise union, and one says to the other, "If you really loved me, you'd—"

Delilah added, "This is the third time you have made a fool of me and haven't told me the secret of your great strength" (v. 15 NIV). You see where this is going, right? Samson may think he's got everything under control, but he doesn't know who he's dealing with.

"With such nagging she prodded him day after day until he was sick to death of it" (v. 16 NIV). She wore him down, and he finally told her everything. "'No razor has ever been used on my head,' he said, 'because I have been a Nazarite dedicated to God from my mother's womb. If my head were shaved, my strength would leave me, and I would become as weak as any other man" (v. 17 NIV). It's not that the hair contained innate power itself, but it was a symbol of his Nazarite calling and vow, meaning Samson had pledged to follow God.

When Samson went to sleep again, Delilah told the Philistines they had one more shot. They came over quickly, shaved his head while he slept, and when she woke him that time, he didn't know that God's power had left him. He tried to do what he always did, but this time it didn't work. The Philistines overtook him, subdued him, put him in chains, and threw him into prison. They gouged out his eyes and made a spectacle of him.

The internal hurricane had wound up full force and Samson crashed big-time. He was called by God and set aside by God from birth to lead his people during a time of great need, but at the end of his life, Samson was blind, imprisoned, and powering the Philistines' grain mill. The internal engine that drove him into illicit relationships with women time after time finally broke him.

You may feel that you are reading your own story. This seems like your script and it makes you a little edgy. In some ways, we've all read from this script, and it sifts out three big questions. These questions are designed to help you take stock of your life. They're indicators that, while you may have made some mistakes, you're not finished yet.

1. God's Power: In Me or Through Me?

Samson was so focused on the external use of God's power that he missed out on the internal exercise of God's power. He was always thinking about what God would do to someone else. He never stopped to think that he had an internal situation that could bring all his plans to a screeching halt. He never said, "God, as much as I've needed your power to kill the Enemy, I need your power to fix me. It's not enough that power goes out from me; I need the power of God to work in me."

Many of us are in this spot today. We know that God can do great things in the world, but do we let him do his great work within us? Strangely, God was still using Samson even during Samson's low points. The man still operated in some of the gifting and empowering and calling that God had placed upon his life even while battling this internal hurricane. If only Samson had stopped to say, "God, I need you to do a great thing *in* me."

When I was in seminary, I worked odd jobs to make ends meet, and one of these jobs was with a house-painting company. The first house wasn't huge, so I guessed our crew would knock off the job in a day. I enjoy painting, but I found out that painting is not all about painting. First, we were told to grab sanders and wire brushes and take off all the old paint. So we worked and worked at sanding. The company owner, building his business on integrity, pushed us to be the best painters in town—and we were in Texas. On that first day, I thought it was about 190 degrees in the shade, and we spent the whole day sanding. I've never been so sore and tired and frustrated, and whatever I was paid, it wasn't enough.

The next day I expected to see a can and a roller. But the boss wanted a little more sanding. He kept saying, "Take it down to the wood, boys." So I was perched on a ladder, hanging on for my life, twenty feet above ground, my hand near some electrical connections, and the boss kept saying, "Take it down to the wood." For days we worked on painting that house and never opened a single paint can. When we finally got to painting, it was done before we knew it. Sure, we could have painted the house in one day. And it would have looked fantastic for about four months before the new paint would have flaked off and left a bigger mess than at the start.

That's a picture of what God is saying to us through Samson. God can do great things, work real transformations, but we need to let him take it down to the heart. We need to say, "God, take my life down to the wood; strip me bare." We'll never be able to do what God purposes unless we let God take away all the facades and rip off all the layers of gunk surrounding our hearts. We need God's power to start working at the base.

2. Sin: Hold Out or Get Out?

Samson thought he knew how to play the game. He wasn't taken out on day one, so he thought he was okay and just kept holding out. He knew he was probably not in the best relationship with Delilah, but bowstrings didn't hold him down and ropes didn't confine him. He still had it. Maybe he knew he wasn't in the best place for serving God, but the loom didn't trap him.

The Enemy, however, was working in his life just like he does in ours: waiting him out. The Enemy is a patient foe and deceives us into thinking we can manage. We assume if Satan can't take us out on night one, he'll give up. But Satan will wait us out for decades if necessary. We need to hear the truth of Samson's story, and it's that we need to get out of the bad place *now*.

Today is your day to get out. You may need to get out of a relationship, a habit, a space you're dabbling in, a valley between God and the Philistines, a middle ground where you've put feelers out. I don't know many people who couldn't understand Samson's life. Most men in some way struggle with sexual temptations.

Today, we have so much opportunity to give free rein to our thoughts. You don't need to go to Gaza to visit a prostitute's house. She can come to your house via the Internet. Women also struggle with sexual temptation, but the focus of Samson's story is on the temptation guys face. The Enemy is brewing up hurricanes, and maybe one of those storms is in you. You may think that because you made it through one day without any dire consequences, you'll make it all the way through your journey. No, that's wrong. It's time to get out while you still can.

3. After a Fall: Laughingstock or Champion?

But Samson didn't get out, and disaster hit. The Philistines grabbed him in his weakened state, gouged out his eyes, took him to their capital city, shackled him, and set him to grinding grain in the prison mill.

They gathered for a feast to celebrate their god, Dagon, delivering Samson into their hands. Dagon was a stone idol worshipped by the Philistines as their primary deity. Later, when they captured the ark of the covenant, they brought it to Dagon's temple. The next day they found that Dagon had fallen face-down before the ark. They set it back up. (Note: if you need to set your god back up because he falls over, you're worshiping the wrong god.) Dagon fell over again, this time with his head and hands broken off (see 1 Samuel 5:1–5). This is the god in whose temple the Philistines staged a big celebration over Samson's downfall.

Here's how the story goes in Judges 16:

> Now the rulers of the Philistines assembled to offer a great
> sacrifice to Dagon their god and to celebrate . . .
> While they were in high spirits, they shouted, "Bring out
> Samson to entertain us." (vv. 23, 25 NIV)

We don't know exactly what this looked like. Maybe Samson stumbled blindly around, and the Philistines thought that was funny. Samson, a man of God, had become a laughingstock for idolaters who jeered and hollered and screamed. You know how it is if you fail in the same area in which Samson failed. When you crash, you feel ridiculous, embarrassed, like your enemy is laughing at you.

Sometimes you feel that way even if it wasn't you who fell. Maybe it was your wife or husband or kids or parents, and you feel everyone is looking at you, saying, "Yeah, that's the guy who did—whatever." The Enemy can make us feel like the whole world is laughing at us, and the Enemy gloats because you're collateral damage. Humans are pretty good at gloating too. We've had to put rules into professional sports to stop this. It's not enough that a player sacks a quarterback for a nine-yard loss; he's going to get a bullhorn and announce to the stands, "Man, I'm taking you out and beating my chest and stomping on your legs and spitting on you and doing a happy dance." The new rules say you can't do that. But as a wounded culture, we love to gloat over the failures of others.

Satan may be dancing on you today with condemnation, shame, and ridicule. "Don't think you're ever coming back from this," he's crowing. He's smothering you with doubt and pushing you into the spiral of continuing sin.

But our God is the God of the comeback. And our God says that even from a low place you don't need to be a laughingstock.

You can be a champion.

A Smashing Comeback

God the Son, Jesus Christ, offers genuine redemption. Have you ever noticed the powerful "but" in some Bible stories? This is the intervening moment. There's always a *but* in God's story:

But the hair on his head began to grow again after it had been shaved. (Judges 16:22 NIV)

Samson's hair started making a comeback, and his hair symbolized his strength vested in the Spirit of God.

The prophet Micah preached to his downtrodden people:

> Do not gloat over me, my enemy!
>> Though I have fallen [true, not to be minimized], I will rise.
> Though I sit in darkness,
>> the Lord will be my light. (7:8 NIV)

The consequences of sin were very real for Samson. He was blinded and condemned to be a slave. But God is always greater than any consequences. The story of God's redemption is for everyone who puts their trust in Jesus for life and for salvation. Satan can knock us down, but we will rise. The real story is that Satan's going down, ultimately and eternally.

We may be left with some scars because we grabbed the low-hanging fruits of temptation, but we're clinging to Jesus, and his grace comes in oceanic proportions.

The apostle Paul tells us:

When you were dead in your sins . . . , God made you alive with Christ. He forgave us all our sins, having canceled the charge of our legal indebtedness, which stood against us and condemned us; he has taken it away, nailing it to the cross. And having disarmed the powers and authorities, he made a public spectacle of them, triumphing over them by the cross. (Colossians 2:13–15 NIV)

So who's the spectacle now? Who's the laughingstock? I may sit for a while in the darkness of my own making, but God is my light, and he is going to plead my case through the blood of Jesus and make a public spectacle of Satan.

Samson's story finishes in Dagon's temple. There the former judge of Israel said, "Put me where I can feel the pillars that support the temple, so that I may lean against them" (Judges 16:26 NIV).

The temple was packed, and there were an extra three thousand spectators on the roof for this major event. Yes, the situation had gone off the rails for Samson. Yes, he had abandoned God's calling on his life and faced the consequences, but he acknowledged that God was still sovereign and still able to make something amazing of his life. In Dagon's temple, Samson prayed. And what a prayer it was!

Sovereign LORD, remember me. (Judges 16:28 NIV)

Isn't that exactly what the thief on the cross prayed in our first comeback story? "Remember me."

Samson continued:

"Please, God, strengthen me just once more, and let me with one blow get revenge on the Philistines for my two eyes." Then Samson reached toward the two central pillars on which the temple stood. Bracing himself against them, his right hand on the one and his left hand on the other, Samson said, "Let me die with the Philistines!" Then he pushed with all his might, and down came the temple on the rulers and all the people in it. Thus he killed many more when he died than while he lived. (vv. 28–30 NIV)

In Samson's last gasp, God's power came back to him. The deliverance of all Israel started the day of Samson's swansong comeback. What he had not done in his lifetime, he did in his death, because our God is the God of the comeback.

That's the lesson for us. It's never too late. We're never too far gone. We haven't strayed too far. God is always good, and he always remembers us. Our prayer isn't to get revenge on a group of people, but it's to be strengthened once more so we might live for God's glory. We push with all our might on whatever stone pillars are keeping us bound. With God's strength renewed in us, the walls of our prisons come toppling down.

SIX

COMEBACK FROM BEYOND

I love college football. Especially if you're talking about Auburn University.

And no comeback collage is complete without us thinking about the "kick-six" in the Iron Bowl grudge match with Alabama at Auburn a few seasons ago. With the game tied, Alabama went for a last ditch long-range field goal to win with mere seconds on the clock. In a flash, the game was decided and Auburn had won!

What no one factored into the equation was that Auburn had placed a defensive back deep in its own end zone just under the crossbar of the goal post. When the kick fell short, Auburn's Chris Davis gathered the ball, darted left, and incredulously skirted up the sideline for a 109-yard, game-clinching TD. And all the people said, "Amen."

This chapter is about a comeback that's even better than a last-second rescue in a big game. Let's start with a big question (and then we'll dig around for an answer): Can you come back from anything—even a diagnosis of death?

When the word from the doctor or the verdict from the judge is a death sentence, is it possible to come back from that?

Tell Jesus About It

Let's dive into John 11, where we find the story of Jesus raising Lazarus from the dead. No matter how many times we hear it, this story has the power to rock our hearts and minds every time.

When Jesus was on earth he did a lot of amazing things beyond his teaching. He healed the sick and fed people from nothing, walked on water and controlled weather. And, Jesus turned death on its head. He did all this to affirm his divine origin and to open the way into the kingdom of God for people who didn't think they had a shot. Along the way he made friends, and this story is about some of them.

The story starts this way:

> Now a man named Lazarus was sick. He was from Bethany, the village of Mary and her sister Martha. (This Mary, whose brother Lazarus now lay sick, was the same one who poured perfume on the Lord and wiped his feet with her hair.) So the sisters sent word to Jesus, "Lord, the one you love is sick." (John 11:1–3 NIV)

We need to understand that Lazarus was really sick. This was not a minor illness or inconvenient ailment; it was a major dilemma and a hopeless situation. The sisters were very close to Jesus, and Lazarus was especially close. Sometimes we picture Jesus as a caricature remote and aloof from people, but he actually stayed in people's homes and ate meals with them and laughed and shared life the way friends do. These three siblings were some of the friends he enjoyed being with. But now Lazarus's condition was so grave that the sisters knew they needed to get a message to Jesus—now!

Jesus was somewhere outside Jerusalem, in the country-side near Bethany (their village). He had work to do there, and besides that, he was a target in major cities. If he showed up in Jerusalem, there were people in the city who would try to kill him, and Bethany was nearby, making it a risky place for him. For the moment he was staying far away. So Mary and Martha sent a message that cut straight to the heart of the matter: "Lord, the one you love is sick." Notice they didn't make any demands; they just informed Jesus. They told Jesus the problem, convinced he would know what to do.

When you get a diagnosis of death, this is exactly what you want—people telling Jesus about it. Have you noticed how many people pray when a diagnosis of death comes? People in the church, outside the church, people who know God, people who don't know God—they all pray.

Recently, Shelley's dad has endured a stem-cell transplant in his effort to battle a humanly incurable form of cancer. Not only are our close friends praying, it seems like everyone who knows us has lifted her father to Jesus. Even people we don't know have joined the cause. Notes of encouragement and hope have arrived from people we have never met and from places we could have never imagined. God has been gracious and we have seen positive results through the grueling process. When some-one you know is up against the odds, you want as many people as possible praying.

Mary and Martha were not just lobbing up a wild-card prayer. They'd seen Jesus do the miraculous. They'd been with Jesus when he had done supernatural acts. They were convinced that if they could get the message to Jesus, then Lazarus's situa-tion would be resolved.

But something changed. Lazarus's story shows a miraculous God doing miraculous things. Miracles are tricky. They're never guaranteed. They're not the norm. But they do happen—and sometimes in the comeback process, a genuine miracle will be called for. Surrounding the narrative of the miraculous in Lazarus's story are four principles that can help guide our perspective with our comebacks. Our first major principle emerges from John 11:4, and it is that God always paints the story on a canvas bigger than we can see or imagine.

1. God Paints on a Wide Canvas

We need to understand this truth before we drill down into the question of whether a person can come back from a diagnosis of death. Let's take a step back from the death question and try to understand what God is doing in the world, broadly speaking. Jesus' words in John 11:4 were not spoken to the sisters but to the followers who were with him at that time, namely, the disciples.

> When he heard this, Jesus said, "This sickness will not end in death. No, it is for God's glory so that God's Son may be glorified through it." Now Jesus loved Martha and her sister and Lazarus. (John 11:4–5 NIV)

We like the feel of where this is going, right? Here's what we have so far:

A. A sickness that will not end in death.
B. God is going to be glorified.
C. Jesus really loves these people.

With those givens—a, b, and c—we expect that "d" will probably be a scene where Jesus rushes up to Bethany and heals Lazarus right away.

But the story takes a strange turn. The next sentence opens with the word *so*. That's not a word we would typically highlight as we study this passage, but it's an important little word. We may have been thinking, "a+b+c = I know what God is going to do now!" But then we get a *so*, and when we hear the word we know things are not going to go down the way we expected.

> So when he heard that Lazarus was sick, he stayed where he was two more days. (John 11:6 NIV)

That's the curveball in the story. The sisters hoped for a "yes," but what they got was a "so." They hoped Jesus would come right then and answer their prayer, yet Jesus stayed away for two days. Remember, God is always painting on a canvas bigger than we can see or imagine. And our second principle is related to the first.

2. Reality Is Bigger than Our Personal Circumstances

Let's take another few steps back and try to look at this from an even wider perspective.

My own family has had to stretch to see this wider perspective when we have gone through some difficult medical journeys over the years. We have faced two life-threatening diseases and have been through years of surgeries and rehabs and hospitals and ups and downs and threats of death and reprieves and times of God's working and little miracles and more waiting. When you step into one of these life tunnels, sometimes everything seems to shrink down to your own circumstances and to the moment you are going through. But God can give you grace to lift your eyes up from your situation, real though it is, to a bigger reality. The truth is that reality is always way bigger than our personal circumstances.

Think of it this way: in the Lazarus story, Jesus is the same Son of God who had left heaven, taken on human flesh, and come to earth. The one who spoke creation into existence is now standing here, experiencing life within the frame of a man. When the sisters' message reached Jesus, he wasn't just lounging by the pool, hanging out. He was doing some serious kingdom business planned before the foundations of the universe. He was just steps away from giving his life for the sin of the world. When this message came to him, the sisters' single frame of reality crashed against his widescreen reality.

The circumstances Mary and Martha found themselves in were significant for them. Their brother was near death. They may have felt like asking, "Jesus, are you getting the message? You've got to come now!" Their facts and feelings intersected with Jesus' huge reality, the reality that he had come to make a way for all people to be forgiven and enjoy a relationship with God forever. It would happen by Jesus' being nailed to a cross to bear the sin penalty for all who would trust in him, as he died both physically and spiritually. He was aware that he would die, be buried, go to the depths, and be raised up by almighty God. That's the reality that was on his mind. That's what was in process. Father, Son, and Holy Spirit were on this mission together, and that's what they were about at the time that Lazarus was dying. This act was to be the ultimate game changer of all time for all people.

Jesus didn't dismiss his friends' reality. It wasn't that Mary, Martha, and Lazarus were unimportant to him. Nor were their problems trivial. But Jesus wanted them to see there was a bigger reality. God is always painting on this canvas that's bigger than we can see or imagine. That's why sometimes a story doesn't play out the way we expect.

We need to grapple with two things within this perspective. First, Jesus did not do what Mary and Martha asked. Second, God wants to use our lives for his glory.

If you've ever been in a moment like that—where Jesus doesn't do what you want him to do—you know how it feels. You put a prayer out there, and Jesus doesn't respond in the way you asked. You don't get a "yes," you get a "so." Understand that you're not the first person that's ever happened to. Jesus did not come to Lazarus that day, and he did not heal him. He did not answer the sisters' request. But he did do something astounding. The purposes of God blend together in the colors he's painting on this big canvas that we can't completely see or fully understand.

And God wants to use our lives on this broken planet for his glory. What's that mean? Sometimes we get tripped up on the big philosophical questions. If God is good, then why is there suffering? Why is there sickness? If God is all-powerful, then why do people die? If God is so amazing, why is the world so broken?

We know the answers to these questions lie within you and me. We are the reason the world is broken. We can blame it on Adam and Eve, but we've done a fairly good job of pushing their agenda forward on our own. We continue to make bad choices, just like they did, do life our own way, and walk away from God's clear guidance for our lives. Just like Adam and Eve, we've also suspected that God hides things from us, so we think we need to work it out on our own to get what we want. Just like them, we continue the willful rebellion of mankind. In this world that's so broken by sin, everything breaks down, and the result is disease and darkness and death.

But even in death scenes, God is painting on a canvas we can't see or imagine, and he's painting a picture with us in it to use for his glory. It's an amazing thing that we can be used for God's glory, and it may happen in one of two ways:

1. He may fix our problem.
2. He may not fix our problem.

That sounds so simple, but we really need to grasp both avenues as part of God's greater overall story.

One way God gets glory is by fixing our problems, sure. God is still able today to heal people supernaturally of any disease. God is able today to remedy any problem we have. In this story, we see the resurrection power of God, and that power is still in effect today. There's nothing in Scripture that says Jesus can't still do today what he did in that day. He could raise the dead and cure us of anything. He can still miraculously restore health and do miracles of any kind. He can do it and sometimes he does.

But we need to grapple with another question: Why does he do that? Why does he heal? We all want to be healed when we get a diagnosis of death. If you dig beneath the surface, we see that our prayers have a simple motivation: *I don't want to die. I don't want my parent to die. I don't want my child to die. I don't want my spouse to die.* That's not a bad motivation, but there's another reason that should go with it. We want a miracle from God so that Jesus will be glorified.

That's what Jesus told his followers about Lazarus' sickness:

This sickness will not end in death. No, it is for God's glory
so that God's Son may be glorified through it. (John 11:4 NIV)

We may wrestle with the question, Did God make Lazarus sick? That's not really a practical question, and there's a better question written over it. Can God heal? The reality is that there is sickness and none of us are immune. But can God reverse those effects? The vital question is, can God heal? And if he can, why would he do so? The answer comes in Jesus' words to his disciples about Lazarus' situation: "It is for God's glory." Yes, God heals, and this is why: so Jesus will get the glory.

It's interesting that sometimes we see God do a miracle and we accept the miracle, but we fail to reflect the glory back to him. Whenever we do that, we lose the blessing. We start thinking our turnarounds are circumstantial, forgetting who is in charge of all circumstances. You may think things just started going your way. You went to rehab and straightened out your life, and some counselors helped, and you got better. You may lose sight of the fact that it was God who delivered you. Think of it this way instead: *I got better and I have a story and I want to tell the world what Jesus has done in my life because I want Jesus to be glorified.* God may use counselors, medications, doctors, and all that, but it's Jesus who heals you.

Here's the other thing we need to grapple with: Jesus doesn't heal everybody. It's simply not his purpose and plan to heal everybody. Now, we could pump this up and say that if we all believed hard enough, then God would do a miracle for every person, but that isn't reality. God never promises to do that.

Some people don't get a miracle, and it isn't because they didn't love God or because God didn't love them or they didn't pray enough or didn't fast or didn't stand on the Word or didn't have enough faith. When you don't get healed, some people and belief systems infer that you must have a chink in your armor, and the devil rammed through with doubt, and that's why you didn't get your healing.

Do you really think that our Father, who loves us enough to give his Son, is on some kind of a faith patrol? "Oh, my goodness, your second cousin showed up from Cleveland with a bit of doubt, and it shot down your whole miracle. So now you're going to die." Do you believe our Father uses a microscope and finds one little place where your faith wavered and then scraps your miracle? No human has faith that doesn't waver, but the Spirit of God pulls you back into hope and faith. I just can't accept that God is sitting in heaven and saying, "Man, if only you'd prayed that prayer a little bit differently, I would have done a miracle." That scene is nothing like the heart of God.

I've been in situations, and you probably have too, when a family oozed faith from every pore, but in the face of their faithful and desperate prayers, their loved one died. Even then their faith never wavered, and they kept on worshiping.

I remember when a young friend of mine faced death. A vibrant voice for Jesus in his generation, family and friends gathered around, Scripture open, and relentlessly prayed to the God of heaven for a miracle. Having slipped into a coma, our friend eventually slipped into heaven, even though his last days were blanketed with faith, worship, confessions of God's miraculous power, fasting, and truth.

At the same time, because God has not promised blanket

miracles in every situation, it doesn't mean we shouldn't ask God for a miracle every time, because we don't know what he's doing on that canvas that's bigger than we can see or imagine.

Sometimes when you're in one of those valleys, well-meaning people don't know what to do, but they put an arm around you and say, "You know the Lord's ways are higher than our ways." Those words are true, but maybe the tone tells you that they've never been through anything like this. They haven't faced what you are facing. But for those who have faced it, we know that God's ways truly are higher than our ways, and his thoughts are higher than our thoughts, and we praise God that that's the truth. God isn't small like we are, and he doesn't see and understand on our small scale. He sees bigger, he knows more, he's doing more—he's running the universe, for crying out loud! He's heading for a great conclusion of history.

Nothing gets in the way of God's great plan. For instance, we had a global economic meltdown a while back that caused our entire world a lot of stress. But it didn't blindside God. God didn't fret one second over our financial market's collapse. In God's reality, that's not even a blip on the radar. He's seen dictators come and go, empires rise and fall, celebrities and nations and decades and centuries and millennia come and go, and he still keeps running the universe. It's not that a radar blip is so small it doesn't matter, but he takes it and works it into his grand plan. He's sovereign over it all. He's working in and through all of it.

Our invitation is to know that our lives can count for his glory. When we go through a diagnosis of death, it's so we can play a part in his big story and glory can come to Jesus. If he heals us, Jesus gets the glory. If he doesn't heal us, that's still for his glory. Either way, it's so we can have a role in the big story of what Jesus is doing on the planet.

The story of Lazarus gives us the most powerful principle of all.

Jesus Is the Resurrection and the Life

The ultimate comeback is to be able to look death in the face and declare that Jesus is the resurrection and the life. When Jesus finally showed up on the scene, Martha came out to meet him and told him it was too late. Lazarus had already died. But Jesus said, "No, your brother will rise again." Martha responded, "Yes, I know he will rise again in the resurrection at the last day." Now that's more than a lot of people know or believe, so we should give her credit for that. But Jesus went further. He said to her:

> I am the resurrection and the life. Whoever believes in me, though he die, yet shall he live. (John 11:25)

It's an incredibly great encouragement to us to know that although God can and does heal, if there's a "yet" in our story and Jesus seems to show up too late and death happens, Jesus offers this wondrous big picture found just a verse later: "Whoever believes in me, though he die, yet shall he live, and everyone who lives and believes in me shall never die. Do you believe this?" (John 11:25–26).

Is Jesus simply saying that Lazarus will come back to life because Lazarus is a believer? Or is Jesus going beyond the miracle of physical resurrection that's about to take place and telling Martha that anyone who is alive physically and believes in him will never die spiritually? Is he raising her sights to a higher truth? Martha believed in a resurrection in the future, at the last day, but Jesus is pointing her to a greater truth—that he is the resurrection and the life in the present. Knowing Jesus is always about life, abundant life, eternal life, and in the case of Lazarus, restored physical life.

In other words, Jesus said, "If you believe in me, then you've come back. Whether you are breathing or not is irrelevant." Read that line again if you need to:

If you believe in me, then you've come back.

Whether you have a terminal medical diagnosis is irrelevant. Your greatest comeback is not to say, "My doctors gave me a death sentence but Jesus healed me." Certainly we celebrate that kind of story and the power of God in it. But there's another story: "A brother received a death sentence, and we walked by faith in Jesus, kept our eyes on Jesus, kept believing in Jesus and praying, and our brother died anyway. Just as Lazarus did. But our dear one just let go of his grip on this life and reached out to take the hand of Jesus to live in the Lord's presence, leaving the body behind." That's a powerful comeback. And on the last day, that person gets a physical resurrection too.

See, even if you are healed from an illness, you'll still die at the end of your life. Lazarus came back from the beyond, but he later died when his time was up. You don't want your whole story to be, "I got healed while I was alive." You want your whole story to be, "I was raised up when I was dead. I was raised up to eternal life when I was spiritually dead in my sins." That's the greatest comeback of all.

Sometimes we try so hard to cheat death, but Jesus wants us to beat death. The apostle Paul said a similar thing at the end of a beautiful chapter about resurrection:

> When the perishable puts on the imperishable, and the mortal puts on immortality, then shall come to pass the saying that is written:
>
> > "Death is swallowed up in victory.
> > O death, where is your victory?
> > O death, where is your sting?"
>
> The sting of death is sin, and the power of sin is the law. But thanks be to God, who gives us the victory through our Lord Jesus Christ. (1 Corinthians 15:54–57)

Do you realize that a doctor could give you a diagnosis of death, you could go through some procedures and treatments, pray desperate prayers, and have people pray for you, and somehow you could get better, but then you could still get to the end of your life and face a future apart from God unless you grasp the grace of Jesus and the victorious comeback he can give you?

The last perspective that lifts up from this story is that whatever situation we are in, Jesus comes to be present with us in the journey.

Jesus Shows Up in Our Journey

Eventually Jesus did go back to Bethany, back to where Lazarus was shut up in a tomb. When he finally got there, Mary and

Martha were shattered. When Jesus saw their tears, he wept right along with them. His friend, their brother, was dead, and that started to emotionally wreck Jesus, too, and so he put his arms around the sisters, and they wept together. It's amazing, because he knew that he was going to call Lazarus back to life in just a minute or two, but still he's with them in the moment. He's fully grieving with them.

When we see Lazarus in heaven, what do you suppose he'll be doing? Will he be parading around saying, "Hey, everybody, I'm the Lazarus from John 11. Yeah, that's me, four days dead. I'm giving a talk this afternoon, and I'll tell you all about the tomb and what it was like to be dead and hear Jesus calling my name, and what it was like to be alive while still tied up in the graveclothes. I'll talk through all of that with you. I'll tell you all about my first little steps out of the grave in Bethany." Do you think anybody would bother going to that workshop? No, Lazarus won't be celebrating that he was given a reprieve from death for a while before he had to live to the end of his life and die. He'll be celebrating because of John 11:45:

> Many of the Jews therefore, who had come with Mary and had seen what [Jesus] did, believed in him.

Lazarus will be celebrating because God received the glory. He'll be greeting the people who came to faith because of what Jesus took him through. He'll be saying, "Thank you, God, for weaving me and my sisters into that story that was so big we couldn't imagine it."

The thing we'll all celebrate together in heaven is that the tapestry will be unveiled, and we'll see how God has used you and me in our circumstances to bring many others into a saving relationship through Jesus Christ. Heaven will be full of the songs of worshipers who had once been broken people in a broken world, picked up and used for God's glory.

A Bigger Picture of Life

My dad was disabled for a long while before he died. Before that he worked as a graphic designer and did a lot of commercial work for Coca-Cola and other companies. He also had a penchant for painting, particularly abstract art.

He painted an amazing abstract of a magician. The whole painting was huge. I'm talking taller and wider than a door. My mom never liked the painting that much. It just wasn't her style. But Dad loved it and wanted to display it. So they reached a compromise. Dad and I cut the bottom off the length of it, and an eight-inch strip off the side. Then he and I reframed the reduced painting and hung it in the landing of the stairwell in our townhouse. Because it was abstract art, it still looked cool—at least my dad and I thought so.

A few years ago, before he died, I was rummaging in the back of a closet in my parents' house, and I found the bottom section of the painting. I pulled it out. Mind you, the cutoff portion was still poster sized. The coolest thing was that it still had my dad's signature, Lou Giglio, on the bottom corner. So I framed it and put it in my office.

The funniest part of this is that, given the nature of abstract art, the picture is difficult to understand at first. I actually thought it looked better upside down. People would see it in my office and make some sort of joke, like, "What in the world is that? It looks like someone threw up on your wall."

I'd laugh along with them and then go poker-faced and act like I was insulted. "Yeah. My father painted that. He's disabled now."

Then I'd smile, clear the air, explain the story, and say, "You know, it's actually a small part of a bigger painting. It's hard to understand it unless you see the whole work." When I looked at the smaller section I always saw the whole painting in my mind.

That's a beautiful picture of how we only see a snapshot of life while God sees the whole thing. We often can't see what our circumstances are about, but God knows. That's who we're called to put our trust in—a God who knows the past, present, and future. A God who's constantly working things together for his glory. We might long for a "yes" while God gives us a "so." But he understands our times and circumstances perfectly, and his times and circumstances are always exactly what we need.

SEVEN

BREAKFAST ON THE BEACH

Putting people on the moon is, no doubt, one of the crowning achievements in United States history. Or, for that matter, any history.

In the early 1960s global tensions were high, especially between the US and the former Soviet Union. The Cuban Missile Crisis had brought us to the brink of nuclear engagement. Soon after, President John F. Kennedy proclaimed that America would put a man on the moon. While something about that idea sounds somewhat ordinary today, it was bold idealism more than forty years ago when a computer would require space roughly the size of a garage, yet possessed far less computing capability than the smart phone you now own.

To get men and a lunar spacecraft into orbit would require a monstrous Saturn V rocket (the launch vehicle that would eventually take us to the moon). But even this magnificent rocket was no sure bet. The Saturn V and Lunar spacecraft were estimated to have close to one million individual components. NASA would only launch with a 99.8 percent "go rate," meaning 99.8 percent of those components were fully operational at lift off. Thus, astronauts were attempting the seemingly impossible with the real possibility that their "ride to the moon" would blast them into space with up to 9,800 things that were not working properly, or at all, at the time of launch.

Not exactly assuring odds.

Risk was everywhere. Not surprisingly, yet tragic nonetheless, disaster struck in January 1967 as three valiant astronauts perished in a catastrophic fire during a launch test less than one month before the scheduled Apollo 1 mission. Our nation was in a race to space, but now the ultimate failure had occurred. Our first manned lunar space flight ended with the loss of three lives without ever leaving earth.

Was it worth it? Would the lunar mission be scrapped? Was the cost of space exploration too high? Was it even possible?

I think a lot of people feel this way. It's the feeling that we once had a shot at God's plans but now we've lost our chance. We failed or someone failed us. Sure, we believe in grace—this wonderful, amazing, life-changing concept that God always forgives. But the truth of grace stays in our heads and doesn't filter down into our hearts. We think that we've blown it or blown it too many times. There's a limit on grace, we insist. Surely God is finished with us.

You have special significance because you are created by God and in his image. And have a unique God-designed calling on your life. A purpose for which you are alive. However, there are a million things that can (and do) go wrong.

Maybe you were called into ministry, yet melted down morally or emotionally or spiritually, and now find yourself driving an overnight delivery truck. Maybe you led a school or a business, yet lost it all because of a decision your spouse made or the betrayal of a friend. Maybe you were hurting emotionally or under extreme stress and a pain pill looked like a way to cope. But now you can't figure out how to face the day without one. Maybe you were falsely accused and had your character assaulted. Maybe you just got tired, or felt forsaken, and quit. Whatever the case, you're now out of the game or struggling to hang on.

JFK's nation galvanizing "moon shot" needed a comeback and it barely had begun. Eighteen months later, in the fall of 1968, Apollo 7 successfully carried three astronauts into orbit. And on July 20, 1969, Neil Armstrong and Buzz Aldrin were the first humans to set foot on the surface of the moon. Due to onboard computer errors, Armstrong recounts he basically landed the Lunar Module by the seat of his pants, overshooting the initial landing site by miles and coming within seconds of having to abort.

The world stood in awe. Yet, Armstrong later told of having less than half the recommended training on the newly designed (and reverse functioning) joy-stick due to the fact that the US was racing to beat the Russians to the finish line. Somehow, with lots of significant things going wrong, NASA was still able to achieve something magnificent.

Remarkable endeavors always require a price. If you've ever set out with compelling and all-encompassing vision—or attempted something groundbreaking—you can relate to this story. Nothing worth doing is easy. All great ideas rise above failure. In other words, comebacks are necessary in every great success story.

So what went wrong on the way to your great endeavor? Have you given up on the possibility of doing something significant with and for God? Are you wondering if you are ever going to lift off and fly again?

If so, you're asking yourself, Can I come back?

John's Surprising Chapter

We've all been there, and I've felt that way myself at times. Yet, I find great comfort in a passage that feels at first glance like it shouldn't even be in Scripture. It's the last chapter in John's gospel. If you're reading the gospel from front to back, it's a whirlwind of action. It feels like the book should really stop at chapter 20, not 21.

The gospel opens with the Word becoming flesh and dwelling among us. A couple of chapters later, Jesus does a miracle at a wedding feast. Then Jesus is talking to a woman at a well and changing her life. A couple of chapters later, he's raising the dead, healing the sick, speaking all kinds of truths, and inviting people into an incredible relationship with God.

Then Jesus gets down to the heart and soul of why he is here. He gathers his followers and tells them he knows what his life is truly about. Then Jesus prays in the Garden of Gethsemane. He's arrested, beaten, deprived of justice, and crucified. He dies. He's taken down and buried in a tomb. On the third day, by the power of God, the stone that sealed the tomb shut is found rolled away and the tomb is empty!

Jesus is alive, raised from the dead. He appears to his stunned followers, even to the doubters. They touch his wounds and see that he's real—even Thomas believes Jesus is raised from the dead—and Thomas is filled with doubt. That takes us to the end of chapter 20, and it seems like that's a good ending right there. Jesus is alive! We could wrap up the gospel and give a huge ovation for the unfolding story of God and the life of the person of Christ. He's come. He's lived. He's died. He's been buried. He's been raised. We're alive in him. It's the perfect ending to a great story.

But along comes an epilogue: John 21. It's like watching a

movie in a theater. After the movie ends, the credits roll, and everyone gets up to leave. Then another scene suddenly flashes on the screen. Surprise! The movie's not over yet.

What could we possibly add to this already great story?

When the Rooster Crows

It's great news for us that there's another act to John's gospel. That's because there's still unfinished business at the end of the life of Jesus, and the additional chapter primarily deals with one man—the disciple Simon Peter—to finish the business. If we look at Peter's life, we see a lot of ourselves in it. Peter was in a world of hurt at the end of the story, and Jesus cared for him too much to leave him with his hurt unresolved.

We need to back up in Peter's story to know why he's so miserable. Peter was the gung-ho disciple. Capable. Confident. He was brash and bold, talking first and thinking later. He wanted to be the greatest disciple, and he wanted to prove to Jesus and everybody else that he was the guy Jesus could always count on. Peter made a lot of promises. He told Jesus he was the guy who had what it takes. Jesus could count on Peter's brawn, sword, zeal, and dedication. Peter even insisted that he'd die for him. Peter looked around at the rest of the disciples as if to say, "I don't know about the rest of these guys—they might bail on you—but I never will."

Ever said something similar to God? "Jesus, I promise you this time that I'm committed. This time you can really count on me. This time I'm going to follow you wholeheartedly. This time I won't mess up."

Strangely enough, when Peter made that promise to Jesus, Jesus basically said, "No, you're not." Jesus wants us all to understand the beauty and wonder of the gospel. He wants us to understand our constant need for the extravagant grace of God. Jesus told Peter, "Actually, I can't count on you. In fact, you're going to deny me three times before the sun comes up and the rooster crows."

Peter's life unfolded exactly as Jesus predicted it would. When Jesus was arrested, Peter followed at a distance. While Jesus was being grilled before the high priest, Peter was outside, hanging around in the courtyard. The night was dark and cold, and Peter and a bunch of people were staying warm by a fire. A schoolgirl was there and recognized Peter. "You're one of Jesus' followers, aren't you?" she asked.

"Nope, not me," Peter said. "I don't even know the guy."

Two more times that night Peter was asked the same question and identified as a follower of Jesus. But again and again Peter emphatically insisted he wasn't.

Then a rooster crowed.

What a moment that must have been. I can imagine Peter wanting to strangle that rooster. It was a moment where Peter was put face-to-face with his own frailties. He saw his own weaknesses up close. He saw his sin for what it was, and I don't know about you, but I feel a kinship to Peter then and there.

I mean, maybe you're the one person reading this book who's lived a perfect life. Maybe you're squeaky clean, and you've got all the perfect attendance certificates and you've never experienced the crushing feeling of embarrassing yourself and letting yourself down and letting God down. If that's you, then God bless you. Send me an e-mail, because I'd like to have you speak at our next conference. Maybe we could have lunch and you could put your hand on my head and bless me with whatever you have that makes you perfect all the time.

Catch my drift? We're all in this together. We all know what it feels like to let Jesus down. We've all made bold promises to Jesus that we've broken. We've all made big commitments to him that we haven't kept. We've all let Jesus down, not once, but many times. We've all been in that moment when the rooster crowed and we came to our senses and realized that we just blew something big time. We can't believe we put ourselves in a compromising position, said what we just did, acted the way we just acted, or crossed a line we swore we never would. That's why the last chapter of John was written.

It's to show us that big foul-ups happen, but Jesus still wants to have breakfast with us.

A Long Night of Nothing

The last chapter of John opens on the shores of the Sea of Galilee. The disciples were all in a boat, and Jesus was on the beach, watching them fish. They weren't in Jerusalem anymore. They were maybe seventy miles away. What's significant about the location is that this was where Jesus had first met Peter three years earlier. But by the last chapter of John, Peter is no longer traveling with Jesus. Peter wasn't helping Jesus feed the five thousand. Peter wasn't helping Jesus heal people. Peter had gone back to the only job he knew.

Catching fish.

What was Peter really doing? When we fall out with Jesus,

it opens a door for the Enemy to blast us to smithereens. Maybe we make a big promise, tell God what we're going to do, tell our friends what we're going to do, or somehow set ourselves up as being someone God can depend on. But at the end of the day, we fail and fall flat on our faces and make a huge mistake and do things we never thought we would do.

That was Peter. By going fishing, Peter was saying that he was finished. He had had his chance at following Christ, but he blew it and denied him three times. We do the same. Whenever we fall down, it lessens our confidence in God. The Enemy comes in to attack and says, "You've let God and yourself down. Don't even bother going back to God. Don't pray about it. God's fed up with you. He won't listen. You've blown it for the last time."

And we believe those lies. The next thing we know, we find ourselves going back to the place we came from. Have you ever whispered to yourself anything like the following?

- I'll just go back to drinking again. I mean, I can't turn to God. What else do I have?
- I'll just go back to this bad relationship. I know this relationship is harmful to me, but God doesn't want me. Where else could I go?
- I'll just go back to my poor thoughts again. I can't ever seem to get a handle on this problem. God's tired of hearing my excuses by now. So I'll dwell on these harmful thoughts like I always do.
- I'll go back to those old friends, back to that old environment, back to the place I used to hang out and to the people I used to run around with. I'll go back to all the harmful stuff I used to do. I'll run to my favorite coping

mechanism because that's where I've always gone for fulfillment and satisfaction. That's where I've always gone to feel better. And even though I never find fulfillment or satisfaction there, and even though I always feel worse there than before, at least it's familiar territory. I'll go back to what I know.

When Jesus showed up early in the morning by the shores of Galilee, the disciples had been fishing all night but catching nothing. Led by Peter, they'd gone back to what was comfortable. But at the end of a night of returning to their old ways, guess what? All they had was a long night of nothing. Have you ever been there? Our culture constantly tells us what we need to do to feel better: party harder, seek happiness in the wrong places, walk the harmful paths. Many of us have gone down that road only to find out it's still not fulfilling in the end.

But Jesus called out to them, "Do you have any fish?" That phrase as it's translated unfortunately misses the impact of what Jesus was saying. The phrase is actually a negative. It's a hypothetical question. The emphasis is placed on what isn't there. A modern equivalent might be, "How's that working for you?" Jesus already knew they hadn't caught any fish—that returning to their old ways was fruitless.

So he offered a solution. Jesus called out, "Throw your net on the right side of the boat, and you'll find some."

To an experienced Galilean fisherman, this advice sounded elementary. I mean, fishermen are fishermen the world over, and if a fisherman isn't catching fish, then he's going to have some sort of excuse for it. The bait was wrong. The visibility was bad. There was cloud cover over the lake. The moon was out of position. The fish horoscope was bad. There's always an excuse. You can picture these guys on the boat all night. They haven't caught anything. They've undoubtedly tried the right side, the left side, the front side, the back side. They've already put the net everywhere! You can almost hear the sarcasm coming from the boat. "Oh, the *right* side! We didn't think of that, did we?"

Who knows their motivation for changing the position of their nets? Maybe they were desperate enough to try what sounded obvious. They listened to the voice, threw their net on the right side, and—*boom*! Greatest catch ever! They couldn't haul the net in because of all the fish.

Let's stay on that point for a moment, because maybe you've been fishing for a long time and have a whole night of nothing. Jesus stands before you, and his message is, "I know where the fish are." Meaning, "I know exactly what you're looking for, and I know exactly where you can get it."

- Jesus says, if you're looking for friendship, I know where that is.
- Jesus says, if you're looking for acceptance, I know where that is.
- Jesus says, if you're looking for meaning in life, I know where that is.
- Jesus says, if you're looking for healing, I know where that is.
- Jesus says, if you're looking for significance, I know where that is.
- Jesus says, if you're looking for security, I know where that is.
- Jesus says, if you're looking for satisfaction, I know where that is.

Right now, he's asking you the same question he asked Peter and the disciples. Jesus is looking at your familiar patterns of living and asking, "How's that working for you?" He's not asking for any information from you. He already knows how it's working out for you. He's giving you the opportunity to form the words in your heart and mind that affirm the reality of what's happening. Once we affirm that reality, then God is able to restore us. As long as we deny our situation and continue to think that what we're doing is great and fun and satisfying and that we're running the show, then we're still under the power of the deceiver.

The moment we speak the truth and answer to Jesus, "Actually, I don't have anything," or "Actually, I feel miserable," or "Actually, what I'm doing isn't helping at all," then Jesus says to us, "Put your net over there." He says, "I know exactly what you're looking for, and I know exactly where you can get it. You find what you're looking for when you follow me."

I love what happens next in the story. When the disciples' net was full of fish, John was the first to recognize that Jesus was on the shore. Peter, always the impulsive one, jumped into the water and swam to shore. The other disciples followed in the boat, towing the net of fish—it was so full they couldn't heft it into the boat. Why did Peter want to get to shore ahead of all the others? He was still the hard-driving disciple trying to work his way back into the graces of Jesus. Peter was still following his old patterns. It's like he was announcing to Jesus, "See those guys still in the boat? They're not swimming to you, but I am! I'm still your guy, Jesus! You can count on me!"

I wonder what Jesus was thinking. Maybe something like, "Man, Peter, do you still not get it? I *can't* count on you. You told me you'd die for me, but you denied me. Three times! What I'm trying to help you understand is that I can't count on you. But here's the good news: you can count on me!"

Someone Jesus *Can't* Count On

That's the core of the gospel, isn't it? Please, let this truth explode in our hearts. It's Jesus saying to Peter—and to us:

- You're not dependable, but I am.
- You're not going to come through, but I am.
- You're going to fail me, but I'm not going to fail you.
- Saving the world doesn't rest on you. It rests on me.

When it came to Peter, Jesus was definitely going to trust him to do big things in the future. Peter was going to be the cornerstone of the early church, and Jesus knew that about Peter. But Jesus also knew that Peter wasn't ready for that responsibility until Peter knew that Jesus was the real cornerstone. Peter needed to be completely clear on that idea. As long as Peter believed it all depended on him, then Jesus couldn't use him. Peter needed to depend on Jesus first.

Here's this same truth taught earlier in John's gospel. Jesus said,

Apart from me, you can do nothing. . . . If you abide in me, and my words abide in you, ask whatever you wish, and it will be done for you. (15:5–7)

Peter had forgotten that. He'd tried to do things his way. He'd denied Jesus. He'd fished all night and caught nothing. But Jesus was teaching this same truth to Peter all over again. Jesus was saying, "You went out and did your thing, but that didn't work. Yet if I just speak one word and point my finger in one direction, and you follow me and my timing and my ways and put the net down where I say put the net down, then look—the net is full of fish."

News flash: this is our same invitation today. It's when we fall on our knees and say, "Jesus, you're the vine and we're the branches. What do you want me to do? Where do you want me to put down the net? Where do you want me to go? How do you want me to speak? What do you want me to be a part of? Whatever you say, Lord, because that's the best way. Apart from you, I can't do anything. So am I fishing in the right place today, Jesus? Am I sowing the right seeds right? Am I investing in the right person? All I want to do is follow you, because apart from you, I can do nothing."

When the disciples landed on shore, they saw a fire with fish on it and some bread. Jesus already had breakfast going for them. Don't you just love a campfire on a beach? It's in this environment of gentle wood smoke and crackling warmth and relaxed vibrancy that Jesus began to speak to Peter. And what Jesus *didn't* say was just as important as what he did. Jesus didn't commend Peter on a fantastic swim from the boat. Jesus didn't chew out Peter for denying him in the high priest's courtyard. Jesus didn't rebuke Peter in any way for failing him.

Jesus simply invited Peter to breakfast.

Whenever we've had a long night of nothing, that's what Jesus does for us too. Jesus asks simply, "You guys want to eat?"

There's no lecture. No condemnation. No rebuke. There's just acceptance. And provision. And a kind of familiarity that only Jesus can provide. "Anybody hungry?" Jesus asks. "Let's eat."

That, my friends, is mercy and grace on display. It's the gospel, and it's the gospel repeated. It's the gospel when we need it the first time, and it's the gospel when we need it the second time, and it's the gospel when we need it the fiftieth time and the three hundredth time and the ten thousandth time. Jesus serves us in our emptiness. Jesus feeds us after we've let ourselves and him down. Jesus welcomes us near and says, "Hello, you look tired and scared and bewildered and beat down and exhausted and burned-out and like you're about to go under. Would you like some breakfast?"

And then Jesus served his disciples. He served them like he serves us. Can I tell you what this is all about? It's about the disciples and you and me losing this idea that we are going to do anything for God. It's about our receiving the idea that God does everything for us and through us. Jesus is alive and loves us and has a purpose and a plan for our lives, no matter what.

After a long night of nothing, after we fail him, this is the sum total of what we're going to hear from him: "Good morning. Come, have breakfast with me. I've got a fire going with some tasty barbecued fish and fresh warm bread, just like you like it. Come, sit down and eat with me, have fellowship with me. Let me feed you and provide for you what you need for this day to come. I am the breakfast for you, because I am life and strength for you. I'm grace for you. I'm power for you. I'm mercy for you. I'm everything you need. I'm here, and I've got it all prepared. Would you like some breakfast?"

A Repeated Question

The story isn't over yet. When Peter and Jesus finished breakfast, Jesus invited Peter for a walk and asked him some questions.

Actually, Jesus had only one question for Peter. But he asked it three times.

Do you love me?

Jesus started by asking it slightly differently. He said, "Do you love me more than these?" (John 21:15). Some scholars think Jesus was referring to the boat and nets and Peter's former way of living, but that's not the most logical way to interpret the question. It's more likely that Jesus was hitting Peter with a question Peter could well understand. You see, Peter was always trying to raise himself above the other disciples. Peter always wanted to be first. He always wanted to position himself as Jesus' go-to guy. So Jesus was asking him, "When it comes to loving me, are you first?"

Peter didn't back down. He said, "Lord, you know I do."

And Jesus did. He knew that Peter truly did love him. He knew that Peter was a work in progress, and for all Peter's mistakes, love was still there. Jesus knew that under all of Peter's bold, brash proclamations, Peter really did love him wholeheartedly, mistakes and all.

So why did Jesus ask the question three times? The more times Jesus asked the same question, the more frustrated Peter became. You see, Jesus didn't want Peter to be confident in Peter and in the answers he gave. Jesus wanted Peter to be confident in God and in God's presence within Peter.

The second time Jesus asked Peter the question, Jesus told him to feed his sheep. And the final time Jesus asked Peter the question, he said the same thing, "Feed my sheep." In other words, Jesus was telling Peter to build his church. Jesus was telling Peter that he wasn't disqualified just because he blew it.

Did you catch that? Because that's what I want for myself and for all of us who've ever wondered if we're ever going to have a comeback.

We're not out.

We're not out because the thing we need most is *not* to be perfect but to be in love with Jesus.

Oh, I can hear the objections already—and some of them are valid. Sure, there are consequences to our decisions, and Scripture says that whatever we sow, we're going to reap. There are consequences for letting ourselves down and for letting Jesus down. Maybe you've made some terrible choices in your past, and now you're living with the consequences of those choices. Those consequences are real and there is no magic eraser to remove them.

Guess what? Grace is more powerful than consequences. Grace overwhelms consequences. Even with consequences there is love and grace and the mercy of God in Christ. Jesus says to us, "I know you messed up, and I know there are consequences, but I want to walk with you through the consequences. I want to love you through the consequences. And I even want to use the consequences in this whole big story."

I don't know the specifics of your story. Maybe your consequences will be miraculously removed or healed or pardoned or restored or smoothed over. Or maybe your story is that God will use you mightily to speak truth and life to people who are experiencing the same consequences as you. The good news is that those consequences don't dictate your life. God is bigger than any consequences. Even if you've denied Christ, he will still serve you breakfast. He will still serve you mercy and love. He will still use you to build his church.

I love how the Bible promises that God's faithfulness is great and his mercies are new every morning (Lamentations 3:23). That means Jesus' breakfast is served and served and served and served and served and served and served again and again. It doesn't matter whatever your night of nothing was about, there is new mercy available every morning. And the meal comes first. Breakfast is served before any problems are sorted out. Mercy is served as the first course. Jesus is saying to all of us that nothing will ever divide us from his love. That includes our failures.

The gospel of grace can feel absolutely scandalous. When we're put face-to-face with the gospel of grace, it seems too good to be true. We think there must be some judgment or punishment or condemnation or court of law or fine we need to pay or ton of bricks to fall on our head. But there isn't. All the condemnation already fell on Jesus. All the penalties were removed by Christ.

All that's left is a breakfast on the beach.

Come and eat, my friends. Come and eat.

EIGHT

GET UP

I wonder if you could point to something in your life that's almost taken you out or is about to take you out. It has you on a stretcher halfway to the grave.

In the time of Jesus, the word *stretcher* was synonymous with coffin. It's what you carried someone on to their burial place. For us, the stretcher can be symbolic of that thing in our life that is carrying us toward death. You're dabbling in something that's opened you to attack and made you susceptible to danger. If you're not careful, that stretcher is going to carry you straight out of town and into a hole in the ground. Maybe not physical death at first. Your death will be spiritual. A death of the heart and soul. The death of a vision. The end of hope.

Maybe it's already happened. The stretcher has already carried you away from the presence and purposes of God.

Maybe that stretcher is a relationship with a person you know is ultimately wrong for you. You love this person, but it's not going to work, and you feel that sense of dread deep down in your gut. You've wrestled the whole thing through in your mind and heart and tried to justify it from every angle, but it's no use. The relationship needs to end. If it doesn't, it's going to carry you away from God.

Maybe that stretcher is a misunderstanding of who Jesus is. You thought Jesus was your buddy. The man upstairs. A friend you merely sing love songs to. Maybe Jesus to you is the meek and mild shepherd who carries lambs and children in his arms—the Jesus you saw pictured in your church when you were young. Or maybe you thought that having Jesus as your personal Savior meant he's a sort of cosmic butler; he gets you things when you need them. Like your slippers or a new car or a great job or a pain-free life. That kind of misunderstanding can lead to your spiritual death.

Maybe that stretcher is your sin. You're living in a pattern of rebellion you know is harmful to you and to those you love. Your sin is overt and public. Everybody knows you're leading a defiant life. Or maybe your sin is quiet, only in your mind and heart. You harbor grudges. You believe the worst about others. You hate. You lust. You insist that your sin is not hurting anybody, but deep down you know you're on a stretcher and heading on the road out of town.

Maybe that stretcher is a wound. Years ago you were hurt. Someone said something or did something to you. You can't seem to forgive, and for years your wound has been festering and growing. You're on a stretcher now, and it's loaded with bitterness, hatred, and resentment. Your wound is leading you to death.

That stretcher of yours could be any number of things: legalism, rage, shame, guilt, intellectualism, entitlement, arrogance, jealousy, disappointment, disillusionment. Whatever it is, you're being carried out of town on it right now. It's only a matter of time, perhaps moments, before you're planted in the ground and covered with dirt.

What you need is a comeback. But not just any kind of

comeback. You need a comeback that saves you from the jaws of death.

No Coincidence

The Bible says that spiritual death is very real. Spiritual death is something we're born into. "All have sinned and fall short of the glory of God" (Romans 3:23).

Spiritual death is also something the Enemy constantly seeks to bring about in our lives. His plan is short and simple. He wants "to steal and kill and destroy" (John 10:10). The Enemy isn't just some sort of caricature to be flirted with. Your Enemy is vicious. He's ruthless. He wants to bury you.

The good news is that something can come alive inside us to get us off the stretcher. It's a radical concept. The gospel is actually a gospel of resurrection power: Jesus stops death. This idea is shown throughout Scripture. Let's take an in-depth look at Luke 7:11–17 together.

Jesus was walking to a small town called Nain, and his disciples and a large crowd followed along. The word *Nain* means "beautiful," and it's a paradoxical image. As they approached the gate to the city called Beautiful, a corpse was being carried out of town. Jesus stopped, interrupted the funeral, and touched the dead body.

So much is happening in this very moment, we need to unpack it. A body was heading out of town, only moments from being placed in the dirt. In those days, the Jewish custom was to have open-casket funerals. The young man wasn't in a box. He was lying on a bier, a simple stretcher made with cloth and two poles and carried by other people. The body was most likely covered from head to foot in burial clothes. It was obvious to everyone in the crowd that this guy was stone-cold dead.

The fact that Jesus interrupted a funeral procession went against the custom of the day. Back then, if you saw a funeral procession heading your way, it was polite either to drop whatever you were doing and join the procession or to cross to the other side of the road and stay out of the way. Certainly a respectable teacher like Jesus should never have touched a dead body; that was against the Jewish ceremonial law. To touch a dead body meant you would be ceremonially unclean for a week.

But Jesus didn't care. He acted outside of his cultural norms and standards. He wasn't worried about what he was supposed to do. He was clear on his purpose and mission—to glorify the Father by conquering death—and he wasn't going to let any taboo or tradition get in the way of that mission. Jesus showed up at the right time and at the right place to cross paths with a person's funeral procession.

This is how Jesus works in our lives today too. Have you ever thought about the incredible odds against your reading this book right now? You could wander into any bookstore today, and fifty thousand books would stare you in the face, all screaming for your attention. Why are you reading this book right now and not one of them? You could click on your e-book reader and literally have ten million books at your disposal. Why this one? Maybe a friend or family member gave you this book. There are plenty of other good books out there they could have given you. Why this title? Maybe you picked up this book at a conference. Or you saw a tweet about it from one of the many people you follow. Or you read a blog post about it from one of the millions of blogs out there.

Why this book? Why now?

It's because Jesus has come to you at this very moment. He's walked straight into your life and straight into your funeral procession. He's walked right over to where you are on a stretcher and he's got a word for you. Jesus is intentional. It's no coincidence that you're reading this book right now. There's something in your life that's put you on a stretcher. That stretcher of death is carrying you straight out of town and to a grave, and Jesus wants to stop that.

What's that word that Jesus has for you?

It's the same word Jesus spoke to the dead man in Nain.

I Say to You, "Get Up!"

All funerals are bleak. But this one in Nain was especially disheartening.

The Scripture says the man who'd just died was the only son of a widow. If you were a widow in those days, you were basically broke. Legally, you couldn't own property or a business. You were dependent on relatives. Most directly, your son, if you were lucky enough to have one. If you didn't have a son or if he died, then you were destined for a marginalized life, certain poverty, and dismay.

That's what this widow was facing. Her husband had died, and now her only son was dead. She had not only lost two of her loved ones, but she was probably going to end up begging for her next meal. She had a broken heart and a grim future.

But then Jesus stepped into the situation. The habit of some Jewish philosophers was to comfort the bereaved with a popular saying at the time: Don't grieve, for it doesn't do any good. How's that for a slap on the face? But when Jesus saw the widow, his heart went out to her and he said, "Don't cry." It wasn't the same thing as what the philosophers said. Jesus said what he did because he knew the future; he was giving the widow hope by telling her to hold on, because he was going to remove the cause of her sadness.

Straightaway, Jesus did something about the dire situation. He walked up to the stretcher and held on to it, enough so that those carrying the stretcher stood still. I don't know if they stood still because Jesus was grabbing on so tightly or if the act of touching the stretcher was so startling to them. Either way, the funeral procession instantly ground to a halt.

That's when Jesus spoke to a dead man. "Young man, I say to you, get up!" (Luke 7:14 NIV). It all happened so quickly. Scripture describes how the dead man sat up and began to talk, and Jesus gave him back to his mother.

I love that there's an exclamation point in the Bible right then. "Get up!" Jesus was reaching with his power and authority into death and commanding that which was dead to be alive again. Jesus wasn't merely hoping something good would happen. He was giving death an order. "Death, you don't have the power here. I have the power. You will obey!"

Immediately the young man sat up. Can you picture that? The graveclothes came loose, and he pawed at the coverings around his eyes. It was like a zombie movie, except this guy wasn't a member of the living dead. He was completely alive, fully restored and made healthy again. Can you imagine the gasp from the crowd? The look on his mother's face? A dead man was breathing again. Their friend was alive!

That's the same word Jesus is saying to you now, the same word he said to that young man. "Get up!" Even though the Enemy wants to bury you, Jesus is in the habit of interrupting funerals. He intersected the one in Nain as well as several others during his ministry, and he can intersect yours with the intentionality and power of the one who raises the dead.

Far too many people think that the power and presence of Jesus don't have anything to do with our lives today. One of the greatest tools of the Enemy is to convince you that Jesus doesn't care about you. Sure, he might have cared about people who lived two thousand years ago. But Jesus doesn't work the same today, does he? A relationship with the living Jesus isn't for you today. You're too far gone. You're too dead. You're too far removed.

That's all a lie! Jesus doesn't let any of that stand in his way. Right at this moment, he is walking up to your stretcher. He's firmly grasping the very thing that's carrying you to a grave, and he's speaking the same words to you that he did to that young man: "Get up!"

That's the gospel in the purest sense. Jesus raises the dead. That's how the story goes. Jesus Christ was crucified on a wooden cross. He hung between two thieves, and the invitation for new life was available to anyone who asked for it even then. Jesus would remember them if they so wished. A feast of grace and mercy was available to everyone, even thieves. Jesus would cover over and take away all the sin and wrongdoings. The cross was where grace was on display, justice was done, and mankind's case was pled before God. Jesus died in our place. Three days later, Jesus was raised from the dead by the power of God. That same power is at work today. Jesus triumphed over death, hell, sin, and the grave. The gospel is about resurrection power. That same resurrection power makes us come alive in the sense that we can be born anew. It also changes our hearts from the inside out. Resurrection power gives us the power to get up off the stretcher and truly live.

Here's how the apostle Paul articulated it:

And you were dead in the trespasses and sins in which you once walked, following the course of this world, following the prince of the power of the air, the spirit that is now at work in the sons of disobedience—among whom we all once lived in the passions of our flesh, carrying out the desires of the body and the mind, and were by nature children of wrath, like the rest of mankind. But God, being rich in mercy, because of the great love with which he loved us, even when we were dead in our trespasses, made us alive together with Christ—by grace you have been saved—and raised us up with him and seated us with him in the heavenly places in Christ Jesus, so that in the coming ages he might show the immeasurable riches of his grace in kindness toward us in Christ Jesus. For by grace you have been saved through faith. And this is not your own doing; it is the gift of God, not a result of works, so that no one may boast. (Ephesians 2:1–9)

Did you catch that? "God, being rich in mercy . . . made us alive together with Christ." That type of resurrection power is displayed when we're saved, and it is also at work *after* we're brought to life. The gospel is so much more than a self-help message. Without Christ, we aren't bad. We aren't merely unchurched. We don't simply need a little help. Without Christ, we're *dead*. And even after we're made alive, sometimes we struggle with our old state of deadness (Ephesians 4:22–24). The Bible tells us to throw off our old deadness and take on new attitudes. Just as we put on a jacket and a pair of jeans, we're to put on our new alive self, the self that's created to be like God in true righteousness and holiness.

You see, being dead is a big problem. If you're a corpse, you can't do anything to help yourself. Not a single thing. So the gospel actually begins with *bad* news: all have sinned and can't do a single thing to improve their standing with God. But the gospel ends with *great* news: through Jesus, the spiritually dead are raised to life. Jesus didn't come simply to make bad people good people. He came to bring the dead back to life. The gospel is about our cold, dead hearts starting to beat again by the power of God. As followers of Jesus, we are resurrected people. Jesus has done for us what we could never do ourselves. By faith, we trust in the death, burial, and resurrection of Jesus Christ to raise us again and give us new life. And when we have this faith, Jesus bursts into our funeral processions and tells us to get up. We're fully alive.

And the gospel continues with the great news. Sometimes, even after we're made alive, we remember what it was like to be a corpse. We're tempted to lie down on our stretchers again. We fall for the lie that it's comfortable being on a funeral bier, heading out of town toward a cemetery. That's when Jesus' resurrection power is still available to us. The same power that raised us from the dead is the same power that helps us walk like people who truly live.

The gospel is not only about a decision you make once and for all; it's about a decision you make every day. I don't mean you lose your salvation and need to get saved all over again. I mean that the gospel is not simply about walking down an aisle or praying a certain prayer or getting baptized later during a different service. The gospel is about living in the light of Jesus' resurrection power every day. It's about who we trust in every moment with our life and eternity.

Think of it this way: we need God's *saving grace* to be made alive. And we need God's *transforming grace* to be made alive every day. The grace is the same grace. The gospel is the same gospel. We need grace to get off the stretcher for the first time. We need grace to stay off the stretcher if it ever beckons to us. And we need grace to get off the stretcher again if we succumb to the temptation of going back to our old (dead) ways.

The resurrection power of God works through us. That's the beauty of Christ's work on the cross. Jesus' work raises us to life and sustains that life until the end of our days. And when we realize that about Jesus, we'll want to respond in a big way.

That's what they did in Nain.

Quietly Worshipful, Noisily Grateful

Here's the funny thing. When all this happened in Nain, the Bible says that the first reaction of the crowd was to be filled with awe (Luke 7:16 NIV). Some translations indicate the crowd fell silent in noiseless worship. It was as if their mouths all fell open at once in a huge collective gasp.

Their next reaction was to praise God. "A great prophet has arisen among us!" they said. "God has visited his people" (Luke 7:16).

You might think the crowd would marvel at the dead man himself, who was now raised to life. Or maybe the crowd surrounded the widow and rejoiced that she wasn't going to be destitute. But they didn't focus on either of those.

The crowd worshipped God. They couldn't stay silent for long. They'd just seen the most amazing of all miracles happen right before their eyes, and they erupted in praise. Some clapped. Some cheered. Some shouted for joy. Some fell on their faces in worship. That's what happens when the Son of God is in your midst and he's calling off a funeral procession, sending an empty burial stretcher back to where it came from.

Here's how Eugene Peterson sums up the story:

> They all realized they were in a place of holy mystery, that God was at work among them. They were quietly worshipful—and then noisily grateful, calling out among themselves, "God is back, looking to the needs of his people!" The news of Jesus spread all through the country. (Luke 7:16 MSG)

That last line shows the result of the miracle: the news of Jesus went everywhere. Don't you love that? The whole thing, I mean. When we're worshiping God, we're seeing him for who he truly is: a God who has the power over everything, even death. When we're together worshiping God, we're invited to have that same sense of holy mystery among us. Sometimes God's work among us makes us grow silent. We find ourselves filled with quiet expressions that go up to God without words. We might be reflective and introspective, stunned and in awe of him. Do you know this feeling? Have you had moments like these where you just want to close your mouth and fall to your knees and raise your hands to heaven in worship?

Yet it's hard for our worship to stay quiet for too long. That incredible place of being in the presence of Jesus brings us to our feet. We stand. We sing. We shout. We clap. We cheer. Jesus is alive! Jesus has all power over death! Something rises inside us until our hearts explode in vocal honor and noisy applause. The Psalmist also described this: "Make a joyful noise before the King, the LORD!" (98:6).

Whether we respond to God with silence or shouts, the result is the same. The news of Jesus spreads far and wide. It spreads among friends and families, from dorm rooms to boardrooms, from conferences to newspapers, from bloggers to conversations over coffee. Jesus' name travels fast, and it's carried by a countless multitude. The message is "Taste and see that the LORD is good!" (Psalm 34:8). The message is "Believe in the Lord Jesus, and you will be saved" (Acts 16:31).

When you climb off of your stretcher, don't make the mistake of thinking that your resurrection story concludes with you. It doesn't. There's more at stake than what happens in your life. What's at stake is how God wants to raise up hope in a community, a nation, and the world to the point where people look around and see what God is doing in people's lives.

Wake Up, Sleeper, and Rise from the Dead

Let's close this chapter in reverence, the type of reverence that recognizes along with the crowds in Nain that "God is back."

To be clear, God never left. He never left the people in Nain, and he hasn't left us today. In Nain, sometimes it seemed like God had been silent for a long time. It had been about four hundred years since the last of the Old Testament prophets were around. The Bible jumped from Malachi to Matthew. But when Jesus burst on the scene and interrupted that funeral procession, the people of Nain recognized the power of God again. That's what prompted them to declare God's return. It felt like the stories of old again, the days of the past when God moved in powerful ways in the midst of his people.

That's what we want to declare today too. "God is back!" No, he hasn't left. But God is here now. The same God that moved in the hearts and lives of people long ago is the same God who works in people's hearts and lives today.

In my work with students, I've been on many of the campuses of the world's largest universities. Each campus is unique and has its own traditions and sports teams and academic profile. But what's always the same are the looks I see on the faces of students as I walk among them.

When I study their faces, I see loneliness. I see heaviness. I see a desperate and sincere need to live for something greater than the here and now. I see a bondage to things that trap people in despair and darkness. I see a spiritual cluelessness that leaves people craving real fulfillment. Walk down any city street and you can see the same thing.

That's why this message is so important. "God is back!" He's working in the lives and hearts of people today. No campus is too far gone. No city written off. He steps into the prison cells of death and proclaims freedom and life. He's the God of the comeback, and he offers comebacks to all who believe.

Remember what the word *Nain* means? "Beautiful." There was a stretcher of death in Beautiful, but Jesus stopped the funeral and turned graveclothes into beauty again.

Maybe you're thinking back to the stretcher you're on, the stretcher we talked about at the start of this chapter. You're thinking that's all you've got, that stretcher of death. You've got stretchers of sin, disappointment, unmet expectations, wrong decisions, grief, and pain.

The message of the gospel is that Jesus loves to interrupt funerals. In Jesus' hands, he turns stretchers into worship celebrations. He grabs hold of your stretcher and tells you to live again. Can you hear the voice of the one who raises the dead? He's calling to you right now:

> Awake, O sleeper,
>> And arise from the dead,
> and Christ will shine on you. (Ephesians 5:14)

God wants to touch your life and use your life to raise up hope for your generation. It's time to let Jesus shine his light of truth and mercy and grace and healing on you. It's time for you to get off your stretcher and walk back into town. It may be that the people who knew you best will stare at you in astonishment and exclaim, "What happened to you?" because they can't believe it. They knew you were heading for the cemetery.

Jesus' message is that there isn't going to be a funeral today. He's the God of the comeback. Let him touch you and heal you and turn your life around. And even if you're experiencing a kind of loss that's pragmatically impossible to come back from, you'll still find out that Jesus is enough.

NINE

JESUS IS ENOUGH

I realize that many stories in this book are about people successfully overcoming obstacles as part of their comeback process. A
person goes from hurting to healed, from addicted to free, from
sorrow to joy, from loss to gain. These stories are powerful and
encouraging. We rejoice with what has been healed or set free or
overcome.

But what do you do when you *can't* come back?

I suspect plenty of people are reading this book whose stories
don't parallel the pattern of a comeback with a happy ending.
If that fits your circumstances, then you feel that tension too.
You know firsthand that whatever was lost in your life *can't* be
regained. Maybe you were finally pregnant but you lost a much-
hoped-for baby. Or maybe you lost your career. Or maybe you
lost a limb in service to your country. Or maybe you lost a spouse
to cancer. In these situations, something won't be restored.
Something won't be like it was. You feel an incredible loss deep
in your soul. What then?

Hold on to that question in all its difficulty while I tell you
about Courtney. She's in her early thirties, a smart, creative,
beautiful, and talented mom of three young kids. She's friends

with both Shelley and me, and she's part of our church in Atlanta. Courtney's story is the story of a comeback that can't happen.

Courtney and her husband, Andrew, were friends in elementary school, then high school sweethearts, and married before they were both twenty years old. Courtney's dream was that Andrew and she would always be together, always be in love. They would even die together in their sleep when they were both ninety-nine years old.

Andrew was a godly man, a great husband and father, and a worship leader at a nearby church. A few years back, on the day before Thanksgiving, Andrew walked out the door to do what he loved to do: take a long ride on his bicycle. Andrew was a serious cyclist and on that day he planned to take a seventy-mile ride. He said good-bye to his wife and kids and left, just as he had done so many times before. Courtney assumed she'd see him again in a couple hours, same as usual. But then the phone rang.

It proved to be one of those calls you never want to receive. One of those radically life-altering, rip-your-soul-apart calls—the type of call that blindsides you with the worst possible news. There'd been an accident, and Courtney needed to come to the hospital immediately. Andrew had been struck by a bus. His situation was critical, and time was of the essence. Courtney hurriedly gathered her children and sped to the hospital.

While she was in her car on the way there, the phone rang again. This call contained the words that shattered her heart.

Andrew was gone.

Courtney walked into the hospital a widow. She could hardly begin to make sense of her new reality. Andrew was never coming back.

The next few days were a blur. Courtney had Andrew's body

taken to Arkansas, where they were from, and she buried the love of her life. After the memorial service, she stood looking down at the grave. Wave after wave of grief washed over her. It was too difficult even to move. A few weeks later, over Christmas, Courtney visited Andrew's grave. When she walked back to the car, she remembered specifically praying a desperate prayer: *God, you've got to help me. I just left half of me in that grave, and I need breath in my lungs if I'm going to make it.*

Hold that story there for a moment and ask yourself what kind of comeback story Courtney would ever have. Wrestle with the tension and difficulty of that question. Her husband was never going to return to her. Andrew wasn't going to come to life again on earth. A huge piece of her life was forever shattered. That was never going to change.

Sure, you could say that her emotions would heal someday, her grief would eventually subside, her life would continue—and that's a kind of comeback.

But in those moments of agonizing grief, when Courtney felt like half her life was buried in the ground, when she had to consciously remember to breathe because she couldn't unless she told herself to, when she ached with every fiber of her being . . . what then?

What kind of comeback can you have when you *can't* have a comeback?

Grace upon Grace upon Grace

I don't want to answer for Courtney.

I know that at intense times such as hers, it's all too easy for friends to offer well-meaning condolences that only sound hollow. I've never been in the position Courtney was, where a spouse is lost. I can't imagine what I'd do without Shelley in my life. I know that I've experienced times of intense pain, times with my dad and mom near the end of their lives, times when I felt so wrecked I had no idea how to move forward. But I can't fully put myself in Courtney's shoes.

And I can't put myself in your shoes either, with whatever deep grief you may be experiencing.

But I can tell you what Courtney told me. I can tell you what I've experienced in my own life in desperate moments. I can tell you what Scripture says. What the living, breathing Word of God holds out for us.

After that desperate prayer walking away from the cemetery that winter day, Courtney returned to Atlanta and walked straight into a Passion conference. She'd been invited by someone in our church who felt led to reach out to her even though they had never met. At that point, I didn't know Courtney, and I'd never known Andrew, although I knew of his passing. His accident had made the news, and I'm a cyclist, so I followed his story closely because all cyclists grieve when there is an incident like his. I didn't know Courtney had come to the conference. She told me later how she felt completely lost when she got there, how she sat down among sixty thousand people, and her desperate prayer that day was the same prayer she'd prayed by the graveside a few days earlier: *God, I don't feel like I can continue. You've got to give me breath.*

That day I spoke in the opening session, sharing a message God had put on my heart for that moment in time. My message, interestingly, was from Ezekiel 37, about God's breathing life back into dry bones. In the text, God brings new life to a place where no life existed.

God asks the prophet Ezekiel, "Can these bones live?" And Ezekiel wisely answers, "O Lord GOD, you know." The implication is that Ezekiel trusts that God knows what he's doing. God can take a stone-cold heart and put a living heart within us. God can give breath where there are only dry bones.

Sometime later, when I eventually met Courtney, she shared with me how hearing that message was a defining moment for her. She realized anew that God was with her in the midst of this raging storm, this dark night of the soul. She knew that God was answering her prayer. God was going to give her breath.

More than two years have passed since the loss of her husband, and it's true that Courtney's life is never going to be the same. She will tell you that herself. Her life is never going to work out as she dreamed it would. She's still living with intense grief, still missing her husband deeply, although she's passed the stage of being numb. Her message is not that her husband has been restored to her. Her message is simply that she has found Jesus to be close to her in her journey.

And her message is that *Jesus is enough*.

That's what I want to unpack in this chapter. This incredibly simple, yet incredibly profound reality: *Jesus is enough*.

That statement acknowledges there won't always be happy endings to our comeback stories—at least not here on earth. Things break in this life and can't always be repaired. Not every story has a happy conclusion on this side of eternity. We don't understand the reasons God allows grief to come into our lives, but it does.

Still, within the journey, Jesus can become enough for us.

And that's the strange sort of comeback that God's Word offers. God can bring Courtney back from her deep loss in a way that only God can define, and the way God is going to bring her back is by being enough for her every day. And God can do the same for you.

I call this *sustaining grace*, a moment-by-moment grace. It's the type of grace that God gives for each and every moment of intense grief, frustration, sorrow, agony, or pain. This type of grace is a tailor-made grace specially designed for each person. It does not transfer over, and it's never repeated exactly the same way, and it's not experienced the same from person to person.

This grace is specific. Timely. Personal.

This is the type of grace that God gives you when you get a phone call that changes your life forever. The shock of the blow hits you so hard, and your mind is a jumbled mess of questions. *Where do I go now? What do I do? Who do I call?* God gives you sustaining grace for that moment.

This is the type of grace that God gives you when you walk down a hospital corridor and know that behind the door is the body of the one you love. Nothing can prepare you for this moment. There's no textbook for this. You have feelings of agony and shock that can't be put into words, and God gives you a sustaining grace for that moment.

This is the type of grace that God gives you on the day you bury your spouse. You struggle to put one step in front of the other. You can hardly breathe. It feels like half of you has been buried in the grave. And God gives you sustaining grace for that moment.

The sustaining grace you receive in the first moment is different than the grace you receive in the second. And the grace received in the second moment is different than the grace received in the third moment. And in the fiftieth moment. And in the two thousandth moment. And every moment after that.

There is a grace for everything. God gives you what you need, and what you need is him. You feel his sustaining grace holding you together. You feel his sustaining grace as you fall apart. You feel this grace because God never leaves you or forsakes you. You feel this grace when you can only be still and know that he is God.

There's a new grace for you when your child doesn't live.

There's a new grace for you when your father dies.

There's a new grace for you on the first Father's Day after your father dies.

There's a new grace for you when you lose a limb to an IED in Iraq.

There's a new grace when you know what's lost isn't coming back.

There's a new grace when what was dreamed is never going to come to pass.

There's a new grace when what was hoped for isn't going to be seen.

This is not a grace that promises you that everything is going to work out for you as you'd hoped.

This is not a grace that offers you any guarantees—except one.

This grace is seldom fully understood.

This grace can hardly be articulated even when it's felt.

This grace is nothing you need to produce on your own.

This grace is what God gives to you when you have nothing left.

This grace is the only hope of the moment, the hope of Christ today, the grace that Jesus is enough.

Little Becomes Big

We see this type of sustaining grace in the story of the Old Testament prophet Elijah and his interaction with an impoverished widow (1 Kings 17:8–24). Elijah had been led on a faith journey with God long before the prophet met this widow, who's only named in the text by her residence as "the widow of Zarephath."

When the story begins, Elijah received word from the Lord that it wasn't going to rain for some time. He walked straight into the royal court of the wicked king and queen, Ahab and Jezebel, and announced the news. As soon as he gave the weather report, Elijah left town. I think Ahab and Jezebel were too stunned at the news to chase after him. Sure enough, the rain and dew were withheld, and a drought came upon the region, and although the text doesn't say so specifically, along with the drought undoubtedly came crop failures and widespread hunger.

Being a prophet in a time of drought was no easy task in that day, particularly when the king and queen were ticked at you. Elijah needed to hide and had no means of providing for himself. For a little while, God told Elijah to camp out east of the Jordan River, along the Kerith Ravine, where each day God provided for him. Elijah drank water from the brook to quench his thirst. And for food, ravens fed him. Yep, ravens.

Picture that crazy scene. Each day, twice a day, a flock of wild birds flapped down and carried Elijah platefuls of bread and meat. That kind of provision only happened for Elijah as far as we know—it hadn't been done before or since.

Note that God used two methods to provide for Elijah in the Kerith Ravine, and one of these was natural and the other supernatural. Anybody could have quenched his thirst from the brook. That was God's natural provision. But the food was supernatural. We can't predict what type of sustaining graces God will provide for us. And we can't expect that the kind of sustaining grace someone else receives will be the same kind of care we will receive. We can only trust that the provision will come.

When it came to God's natural provision, even that was no easy thing for Elijah to handle. I imagine myself in Elijah's shoes, looking at that brook day after day after day. He knew that water was becoming scarcer and scarcer as the drought continued. Each day the brook was a little lower and a little lower. Did Elijah ever panic? Did he ever do the math to figure out how much time was left?

It wouldn't have been hard to do. And that's a truth I need to learn over and over again in my own life. *Be wary of the math!* It's easy to look at a natural source of provision, particularly when the water's going down, and worry that it's the only way God will provide for us. In the process of nervously watching our water supply dwindle, we look around at all we still need to do or all that we feel called to do in the future, and then we look only at the natural provision we have. And that doesn't look like it's going to be enough. The water's running low, just about finished, and when that happens, we're done. There's no way we're going to be able to function after the brook runs dry. Right?

We forget that while the brook is going down, God is still bringing us bread and meat by ravens. The miraculous is always happening, even though we forget it or even when our faith is too small to trust God for miracles or even when we don't see the miracles occurring. God is always still at work, and God will always provide for us. Whenever the brook runs dry—and it will—God will provide another sustaining grace for us. We don't need to worry. We can be thankful that we have a sustaining grace now, and we can be confident that another sustaining grace will come later. Jesus *is* enough, and Jesus *will be* enough.

Sure enough, in Elijah's case, both the natural and supernatural provisions ended—at least in as far as he could see. The brook dried up. The ravens stopped coming. At that point, the sustaining grace of God changed for Elijah. God told Elijah to travel to Zarephath, where a widow would take care of him. This widow wasn't rich—we can see that right away in the text. She had one son, and their food was also running dangerously low.

The fact that God's provision would come from a widow should make us all scratch our heads. Why a widow? Why didn't God send Elijah to a wealthy benefactor? To one of the city rulers maybe? Or maybe to a family with an abundance of food? It's a strange directive, and it makes me think of the kind of provision shown in the story of Jesus and the feeding of the five thousand (John 6:1–14).

In that story, Jesus had ministered to a huge crowd all day. By nightfall, it was time for a meal and everyone was hungry, but the crowds were still hanging around on the Galilean hillside. Jesus asked his disciples where they were going to buy bread for the people to eat, and nobody had an answer. Philip, the practical disciple, noted that it would take more than half a year's wages to buy enough bread for each person to have only a bite. The task couldn't be accomplished by natural means. Then Andrew spoke up and mentioned there was a small boy nearby with five barley loaves and two fish.

A small boy with a box lunch? That's the solution? Sheesh, Andrew, got any more bright ideas?

But that was more than enough for Jesus.

You see, Jesus isn't the God who looks at the overabundance of the world's wealth and sees that as the answer to all the world's problems. Instead, he looks in unexpected places. At widows and small boys with box lunches and the poor and the downtrodden and the meek and those without power and those for whom life hasn't worked out as hoped. Jesus sees great value in them.

Jesus' answer is not to *take* from them. He *invites* them to places of prominence and importance in his overall story. God looks at the people who are poor in the things of the world and says, "Do you realize how incredibly important you are? You don't think you have any might or power, but that's not how I operate. I operate by the might and power of my Spirit. And when I'm operating by the might and power of my Spirit, there's no end to what can be done."

That's what Jesus used. He had everyone in the crowd sit down. He gave thanks for the meal and began to distribute the food. He blessed the bread and broke it. Suddenly there weren't just five loaves and two fish anymore. Suddenly there were ten fish and fifteen loaves. Then there were fifty fish and a hundred loaves. Then there was bread everywhere. Loaf after loaf. And fish. More delectable fish than anyone could pass around. Everyone ate and ate and ate some more. When the feast was over, there were twelve basketfuls of leftovers—enough for everyone to have a late-night snack or breakfast the next morning or to take home for future provision. I like to imagine the little boy after the meal, the boy who'd given his lunch away. How full was he afterward? How round was his belly? How much food did he take home in his lunchbox? What kind of abundance did he have *after* he gave everything away?

Jesus isn't dependent on natural provision. If we need

something, as a matter of first things first, we don't need to ask the people who have enough if they will provide for us. Corporations and rich people aren't in charge of the kingdom of God. God told Elijah to go to the widow of Zarephath because he wanted to demonstrate the same truth to Elijah that he would later demonstrate to the crowds who were fed by the five loaves and two fish. Jesus himself was the Bread of Life. Jesus was all they really needed!

Jesus even said this about himself: "I am the bread of life; whoever comes to me shall not hunger, and whoever believes in me shall never thirst" (John 6:35). The miracle is that Jesus provides true bread for us. He is the true sustenance we need.

That's exactly what happened with Elijah and the widow. The prophet found the widow outside Zarephath, near the town gate. He called to her and asked for a little water in a jar and a bit of bread.

"Well why not," she said, or words to that effect. "All I've got left is a handful of flour at home and a little cooking oil in a jar. Here's the big news, Elijah. I'm going to use these little scrubby sticks I'm collecting to build a fire when I get home. I'm going to use these last scrapings of my oil and flour to bake one last tiny meal for me and my son. We're going to eat that, and then we're going to die. I'm at the end of my rope. My brook dried up a long time ago. You want the last of my food? Why not? If I give it to you, then all that does is hasten the end of our misery."

Have you ever been there? At the end of your rope? How crazy does it sound that when we are at our absolute lowest, God asks for something from us? He invites us to give him our last meal. Do you know what that meal represents?

It's our full trust.

When we are at our absolute lowest and weakest, Jesus invites us to hand him everything we have left. He invites us to give him our little, whatever our little is. When we give away our little, we place our full confidence in him. After all, it makes no sense to cling to our last meal anyway. As soon as we eat it, we'll be finished. We may as well place our last meal in God's hands. Take our chances. What's the worst that can happen?

On behalf of God, Elijah made that request of the widow. He said to her:

> "Do not fear; go and do as you have said. But first make me a little cake of it and bring it to me, and afterward make something for yourself and your son. For thus says the LORD, the God of Israel, 'The jar of flour will not be spent, and the jug of oil shall not be empty, until the day that the LORD sends rain upon the earth.'" (1 Kings 17:13–14)

She went and did as Elijah had told her, and sure enough, there was food every day for Elijah and for her and her son. The jar of flour was not used up, and the jug of oil did not run dry. She gave away all she had, and she ended up with much more.

This experience is so similar to the little boy with his loaves and fishes. He gave away all he had, yet he ended up with more, not less. That's God's math. That's God's great economy. Start with a little and give that away and you end up with a lot. How often do we sense this same request of God in our own lives? The question's not as easy to answer as we might think. We worry that if we give our little to God, we won't have anything left. We don't want to give our little away. Have you ever been there?

We fear that if we give our all to God, he will take away our dreams. He'll make us missionaries in the deepest, most remote jungles of Africa, where we'll languish in obscurity and dysentery and insignificance.

Or if we give our tithe to Jesus, we're not going to have enough. We won't be able to pay our bills; we won't be able to make this month's rent; we won't be able to get a car or a shirt or a computer or a guitar or an engagement ring or whatever it is we need.

Or if we place our last final emotion of grief or rage or pain or agony or loneliness or disappointment into the hands of Jesus, we won't be able to feel anything at all. We'll be completely numb, and we desperately want to feel something, anything, even this pain we're holding on to with all we've got.

We fear that if we give our all to God, we won't have anything left. But Jesus offers these powerful words that sound so counterintuitive to us:

> Whoever would save his life will lose it, but whoever loses his
> life for my sake will find it. (Matthew 16:25)

Jesus is telling us that whoever wants to save his all will actually lose it. So there's only one solution. Give it away. Give God your dreams. Give God your intense feelings. Give God your little and see what he does with it. If the widow had kept her last oil and flour for herself, how long would she have lived? If the boy had held on to his loaves and fish, what would he *not* have experienced?

Have you put all you have and all you are and all you hope for and all you can ask for and imagine into the hands of Jesus? When you do, you will find something that the widow at the end of her rope found. You will find what the disciples and the small boy and the crowds on the hillside found. You will find what Courtney found after the death of her husband.

You will find that Jesus is enough.

A Strength and Portion

What does this phrase "Jesus is enough" actually look like in practical everyday life? Sure, it means we have nothing except Jesus, and all we have is his sustaining grace. But what might that actually look like for us?

When Jesus is enough, we might not actually be poor in the things of this world. We might be relatively wealthy and have cars and houses and college tuition and loving family members and a full refrigerator and a fulfilling job and an abundance of hobbies and clothes and bank accounts and an embarrassment of first-world blessings. And yet we know that if it all disappeared in the next five minutes, Jesus would still be enough.

When Jesus is enough, we might be like that small boy. We have our health and strength and a bit of provision and dreams of growing up and doing cool things and being a great agent in God's kingdom plans and a loving spouse and a caring parent. And we've just been hanging out all day, listening to Jesus, which has been great. And maybe there's a need placed right in front of us. We know we can't ever fill the entire need, because that would take more than all of our resources, maybe half a year's wages, and even then the need wouldn't be filled. But we can still give away our lunch. We can give what we have. We can place our loaves and fishes into the hands of Jesus and trust that he will do with our offering whatever he wants to. That's when Jesus is enough.

When Jesus is enough, we might be like the widow of Zarephath. The brook has run dry. The crops have failed. The oil and flour are gone. We have nothing left, and our hope is gone. All we can do now is eat a last meal and then die. If that's your story, you can rest assured Jesus is extending a huge invitation to you: give him your all. If Jesus is your all, and if Jesus is all you have left, then that's what it means that Jesus is enough.

I love how the Psalmist articulates it. He has grief in his heart and he's experienced trouble after trouble, yet even at the bottom of life, he says to God:

> *Whom have I in heaven but you?*
> *And there is nothing on earth that I desire besides you.*
> *My flesh and my heart may fail,*
> *but God is the strength of my heart and my portion*
> *forever. (Psalm 73:25–26)*

That's the cry of someone who knows that Jesus is enough.

When Jesus is enough, we focus on what we have, not on what we don't have, and not on what we still might lose. When Jesus is enough, we bless God and don't curse him. When Jesus is enough, we gaze intently on God and run to him, not away from him. When Jesus is enough, we believe God and don't doubt him, even though we don't understand our circumstances. When Jesus is enough, we ask him to take the half of us that's left and make that everything he wants us to be. When Jesus is enough, we realize our hearts were made for Jesus, and Jesus isn't just a theological idea—he's a person and not just any person.

He is *the* person our hearts and souls were made for.

That's when Jesus is enough.

No Easy Answers

There's one more question that comes to mind when trouble comes our way. It's the big question. Why?

Why did Courtney's husband die?

Why did the widow of Zarephath reach the end of her earthly provisions?

Why did my father become so ill and suffer so much toward the end of his life?

The big answer is that we don't know. We will never know all the mysteries of God and how he works within a broken world for his glory. That might sound like an overly simplistic answer, but it's not. It's an answer full of trust. It's an answer full of pain and the realities of a broken world, and it's an answer that's full of hope.

We know, because of Colossians 1:15–17, that all things were made by Jesus and for Jesus, and in him all things hold together. That means we were uniquely made by Jesus and that each of our lives was uniquely created for his purposes.

God is never far from any one of us, and sometimes he allows our lives to be stripped down to the bones so we can reach for him and find him. When things are going great, it's far easier to forget God. When our deals are going through, when our Facebook page is active and we're getting a lot of likes on each post, when our relationships are smooth, when our bank accounts are in the black, when our health is good, when our children and friends are happy, when we're doing well—that's when it's hardest to be closest to God. But as soon as that great job is lost or relationships fragment or when someone we love is hurting or dying, that's when we look to heaven and call on God.

Sometimes God in his sovereignty will strip away those earthly things we cling to hardest to get us back to the epicenter of our existence, that we would seek God, reach for God, find God. The times when life is difficult are the times when we make the most progress and see the most expansion in our personal relationship with God.

The good news is that we always find a God who's sufficient, relatable, and dependable. He's the satisfier. Our flesh and hearts may fail, and all the things we think will fill our life may fail. Our friends will flake on us. We might even let ourselves down. But God is our portion, or as the Psalmist says: "God is the strength of [our] hearts" (73:26).

God often meets us most powerfully when we are willing to admit that we don't have the resources to move past the moment we're in. There is no Plan B. We have no strength left. We've run out of all human options. That's where the miracle happens.

That's the comeback for us when we have no comeback. Jesus supplies us with what we need for the moment, for the day, for the season. And then he provides another grace after that and another grace after that. Grace isn't a one-time deposit. It's a moment-by-moment relationship with God, where we trust Jesus to be in us and through us and for us. We trust that he will come through in his own time and in his own way.

When we have no comeback, the comeback is that Jesus is enough.

TEN

A VISION ON A PLANE

The big idea of this book is that at some point everybody needs a fresh start, a change of direction, a spiritual turnaround, a new beginning.

So what about you? Have you had one? Do you need one? Are you walking through life right now with someone else who does? If so, what might your comeback look like? Can you imagine it right now? Can you see where you'd like to end up, a place that's different than where you are right now?

If the answer is yes, that's super encouraging to me. It says you are still alive. Still hoping. Still believing. Still trusting God's not through with writing the story of your life. Maybe the cry of your heart is *Lord, please use me in the best way possible.* And that's fantastic!

But be assured. God's plans rarely mirror ours.

I'm always reminded of the day God led his people out of bondage in Egypt toward the Promised Land. He did not lead them the shortest route; he led them straight into the desert. Sound familiar? We see a dilemma in our lives, quickly assess the situation, come up with a solution, and then inform God and wait for his intervention. But then God not only does not do what we suggest, he does the opposite.

But when he does this, God is still good and glorious. God knew the shortcut would be laden with challenges the Israelites were not yet ready to face, so another plan was set in motion.

> When Pharaoh let the people go, God did not lead them on the road through the Philistine country, though that was shorter. For God said, "If they face war, they might change their minds and return to Egypt." So God led the people around by the desert road toward the Red Sea. (Exodus 13:17–18 NIV)

For their best, God led his own into the wilderness. Wow. So what was the big blessing waiting out in the barren desert? Hang on to that question for a moment.

———

When I was younger, people always talked about how you needed to have a five-year plan, a ten-year plan, and a solid direction mapped out for the future. We often feel pressured that we need similar predeclared plans in place today. But the longer I walk in my journey with God, I've discovered that five- and ten-year plans in his economy are not what I used to think they were—a sure-bet direction for life. Discovering God's prepackaged plan isn't really what's on God's heart for you today, because God isn't interested in giving anyone a detailed road map to life, certainly not one that drops down out of heaven in a FedEx envelope.

Actually, God has something better for each of us. The big truth we need to grasp is that God loves us. It's a personal and individual love. In that love, he has specific plans and purposes for each of us. The plans God has for me are not the same as the plans God has for you. And the plans God has for you are not the same as God has for me. Our aptitudes and experiences and skill sets are different and unique. I'm not wired exactly like you, and you're not wired exactly like me. God has a personal plan and purpose for each individual.

What we end up doing too often is looking at other people and saying, "Wow, I wish I were more like him." Or her. Or them. Or that group. Or that project. Or that mission. Or that institution. Or that artist. Or that leader. But God is saying, "Don't be more like him or her or anybody else, because I took care to make you exactly like you."

Though we are all made differently, we have something massive in common. The most important thing that's wired into each of us is that we all have an ability to have a relationship with almighty God. Stunning. Can I say that again?

We all have an ability to have a relationship with almighty God.

We're talking about the God of the universe, and this ability to have a relationship with him is the most important thing about any person. God is far more interested in developing that relationship with you than he is in giving you a concrete, detailed blueprint for your life.

That's precisely why God *isn't* in the habit of giving blueprints. It's because God wants us to constantly lean into a relationship with him. The moment we feel like we have a blueprint, we think, *Okay, this is all I need. I'm off and running. Thank you, God. See you later. I know what I'm doing. I know where I'm going. I know how and when it's all going to fall into place. So let's go. I'll check in if I run into any big obstacles or need your help. Thank you very much.*

No, God is less interested in handing us long-range, detailed plans and more interested in cultivating a personal, day-to-day relationship with us. Before we go too much further, let's not make the mistake that plans don't matter—that God doesn't want to plant us in fruitful vineyards and teach us how to commit to a mission, task, or relationship for many seasons. It's just that as we follow Jesus, life is far less predictable than we figure it's going to be.

God wanted to grow the faith of his people. Not in their ability, but in his. Thus, the desert classroom was the greatest environment possible for them to learn that he would always be more than enough—no matter what. In the unpredictable places in life, we learn that the one thing we can predict is that God will come through.

And when our comeback arrives, it will almost always look different from what we first imagined. This is exactly what God wants for us. He doesn't want *our* dreams. He wants *his* dreams. He doesn't want us swimming in a kiddie pool of faith, a faith that's only ankle deep. That's a faith with no risk involved, a faith where we can still touch the bottom. God doesn't want an easy road for us. No shortcuts. Instead, God wants to take us on an adventure far out into the widest part of the ocean. He leads us into deep waters where there's no way our feet can touch bottom anymore. That's when we lean on God and constantly seek his face and heart and thoughts, because there's no way we can ever swim in the deepest part of the ocean unless we know the one who holds the seas in the palm of his hand.

When God is writing the story of our comeback, we can have confidence that the comeback he brings is the exact comeback we need. Since he's the God of the comeback and because he's always good and glorious and always cares for us, the comeback he brings will be better than anything we could ask for or imagine. You see, when God looks at you, he doesn't think things like "average, ordinary, or lowest common denominator." Instead, he's thinking, "I want to take you on a grand adventure where whatever you're dreaming about is not big enough. Whatever you're thinking about is not wide enough. I am God, and you and I are going on an epic journey in life beyond all you have imagined." That's the way God thinks about your life.

Can you get your mind around that? Would you be willing to step into a place with God where you let go of your future as you imagine it? Are you willing to let go of the plans you have for your life and trust him for his? The prayer here is, *God, whatever you have in mind for me, that's what I want to be a part of. Whatever you're thinking about, that's what I desire.*

To get there, the road often takes some unexpected turns.

Big Confusion—Big Frustration

I mentioned earlier that my dad was suddenly disabled in midlife.

In the mid-1980s, I found myself a long way from home in grad school at Baylor University in central Texas. You could say I went there after my first grad program in Fort Worth due to my fascination with church-state studies, and the fact that at the time, Baylor had a world-renowned church-state program. Saying that would be true. But you could also say I was miraculously drawn there because my soon-to-be-wife was finishing her undergraduate studies at Baylor. That would be true, as well.

I thought I'd be there for two years. That was my plan—two

years at Baylor. Shelley and I would finish our programs, get married, and then God would lead us off on some grand ministry adventure somewhere in the world.

That was our *direct* route.

Turns out, we ended up staying at Baylor for ten years. Not in school, mind you. God had another plan.

When I arrived at Baylor in the fall of 1985, Shelley and I started a weekly Bible Study, gathering students in worship and the Word. We started with a handful of other students who were friends, yet quickly our little clan became one of the largest weekly campus Bible studies in the world at that time. After a few years, fifteen hundred students were gathering on Monday nights packing into whatever venue we could find. On any given week, that represented more than 10 percent of the campus population. It was, in our estimation, the wind of God.

Just a few years in, while we were in Colorado skiing with Shelley's family, my mom reached me by phone. My dad had suffered a seizure in Atlanta and was in the ICU. The details were sketchy. She didn't fully understand what was happening with his condition and, thus, we didn't either. All I knew was my dad was in a coma. Everything else was uncertain.

We soon discovered a life-threatening virus had attacked my dad's nervous system and death was on the horizon due to severe infection and swelling of the brain. The only solution was immediate decompression surgery where a portion of my dad's brain would be removed to allow for more swelling without fatal consequences. Without the surgery it was likely he would not live through the night.

Having flown home to Atlanta, I remember staring across the small consultation room at my mom and the surgeon. On the table was a piece of paper that would authorize the procedure that would spare my dad's life. Time was of the essence. The situation was critical. We asked all the questions we could think of. But that's the problem. We couldn't really think.

Nowhere in my life's plan did I envision myself at thirty-one signing a form giving consent to a doctor I had never met in my life to remove a section of my dad's brain.

Within hours surgery was underway.

Thankfully, my dad came through the surgery that night. During the hours-long procedure, I had investigated and scoped out the route they would take my dad from the operating theater back to ICU. Camping out against the wall in the hallway, I got six seconds with him post-recovery as they hurriedly wheeled his hospital bed across the passageway.

"Dad, I love you. You're doing great," I barely blurted out as our eyes met, trying my best to lift his hopes.

But damage from the presurgery swelling, and a subsequent stroke a day or so after the operation, left him disabled mentally and physically for life. For our family everything suddenly changed.

My dad, whom I loved so much, went from being a highly successful graphic designer and a bona fide genius to a guy who spent his days needing around-the-clock care.

For the next seven years, we all adjusted to a new way of life. Shelley and I remained in Texas (though I prayed a hundred times God would let us go to Atlanta), while Mom shifted more and more into the role of primary caregiver for my dad. Shelley and I came and helped whenever we could. Over time, there were brighter days mixed with setbacks, additional surgeries, and a lot of dark nights. Seeing him like that crushed me. There were nights I was with him in the hospital (a follow-up brain surgery, a broken hip from a fall, a broken back from a car accident on a trip to the doctor, and more) and he was so despondent and miserable. I'd pray that God would take him home. My mom, who was nothing if not honest, would often say, "There are things worse than death." Life had shifted. Permanently shifted. And while Dad was getting the best possible care, we thought we were losing Mom.

But any time Shelley and I prayed about moving—and we prayed about it a lot—we got a no.

In many ways it was a confusing time spiritually for us. Not in the sense that we didn't believe God or believe his Word. But in the sense that we wanted to do the right thing by helping my mom and dad. God impressed on us that we needed to be in Texas. In particular, for the last four years we were at Baylor, we prayed earnestly that God would clear the way so we could leave our ministry and move to Atlanta. Other people were praying about this decision with us—mentors and people we respected greatly in the faith. Yet, the answer was no, and the answer was strongly no. So we stayed. And God blessed our little tribe and the Bible study continued to grow.

Finally in the winter of 1994, after ten years at Baylor, things changed. I had taken a weeks-long sabbatical break after the fall semester, and in the last few days I sensed in my spirit a release from our work with the students at Baylor. Shelley agreed. We were free to help my mom care for my dad. Shelley and I didn't have jobs in Atlanta. We didn't have any blueprints of what to do. But we knew that was God's direction for us, so we transitioned out of our ministry at Baylor—handed it over to other leaders and made plans to move. The only thing we knew to do was help my mom and trust God for the rest.

Fast-forward to Monday night, May 1, 1995, the last Bible

study we held at Baylor. The school year was coming to a close and our time at Baylor was done. This night was to be the celebration point. The thank-you event. The big send-off for Louie and Shelley for a job well-done. Former students came. Our board of directors came. It was a big deal—all except for one thing.

Shelley and I weren't there.

On the same day (the day of our final Bible study after ten years), we buried my father. He had died three days earlier on Friday morning, April 28. He died of an unexpected heart attack, which wasn't related to his disability. While everyone at the Bible study was celebrating all God had done there, we were in Atlanta at a funeral. They sent us a video later.

The crazy thing was that our only reason for moving was now gone. At least in our way of thinking. We'd officially resigned. We'd said our good-byes. Other staff were in place. That season of our life was now in the rearview mirror.

And frankly, the windshield through which we were looking for the future was shattered.

I was a wreck. I was grieving for my dad. I felt crushed and confused. I try not to overstate it now, but I was frustrated, maybe the most frustrated I'd ever been. We went through with the move to Atlanta, but we had no idea what to do. We felt like we were in no-man's-land. I wondered if maybe I'd misread God's will. Maybe we were supposed to move back in November when I'd first sensed God releasing us to move, and not in May when the school year was complete. I didn't second-guess God, but I second-guessed what I'd heard and how I'd responded to it.

We were at a low point. Confused. Questioning. Shaken.

We didn't even know it at the time because we were in a fog of uncertainty. But what we needed was a comeback.

Four Tasks in Waiting

Hold on to that tension, because I'm going to come back to it at the end of this chapter. There's a passage of Scripture that means a lot to me as I reflect on these events in my life, and I want to share it with you first.

> Trust in the LORD, and do good;
>> dwell in the land and befriend faithfulness.
> Delight yourself in the LORD,
>> and he will give you the desires of your heart.
> Commit your way to the LORD;
>> trust in him, and he will act. (Psalm 37:3–5)

Read that passage again if you need to, because there are four phrases I want to touch on—four tasks for us to do while we wait—and they relate to our lives in big ways. When we're wanting to know the outcome of a comeback before it happens, and the outcome isn't revealed, this passage offers great perspective.

The first task is simple.

1. Trust in the Lord, and Do Good

That task calls us away from any panic we might feel.

When we start to head toward a comeback, we think we need to have our destination figured out. We're not sure how it's all going to play out, and we can't figure it out. So we're overwhelmed.

Much stress is lifted from us when we come back to the starting place—the basic foundation of truth—trusting in God and doing good. People are going to scrutinize us by asking, "What are you going to do?" "Have you figured it all out yet?" The place to start is to answer, "I've decided to trust in the Lord and do good. I'm not 100 percent sure where all this is going to go, but I'll tell you that I'm actively trusting in the Lord."

Trusting is never passive. When we trust, we don't just sit back and chill. In the waiting mode, in the journey of heading toward a comeback, the invitation of God is to keep doing the very best at whatever God has put in front of us. This means we adopt the attitude of relying on a great and sovereign God to orchestrate the plans and purposes and direction of our lives.

When our view of God expands so we can see him as he truly is—as a big and extraordinary God—we have less need for specifics. We've seen God act before. We trust him for how he's going to act in the future. We're not stressing out over what he can and can't do. We know we're loved by him and called by him and chosen by him and created by him. And if all those things are true, then God is going to lead us into his best purposes and plans.

I love the story of the patriarch Abram. (That was his name before it was changed to Abraham.) He was faithful to God even before the cross, and his faithfulness was counted to him as righteousness.

Abram lived with his family in a place called Haran. In Genesis 12, God said to Abram, "Go from your country and your kindred and your father's house to the land that I will show you" (v. 1).

That was God's revealed plan for Abram. Period. Only that much. Just pack up and roll on out, and as you're going, I'll show you where we're going to go. The leading wasn't to the land I *have* shown you. It was go to the land I *will* show you. This is often the way God leads his people even today. *Step out of the boat, and walk toward me on the water. I'll show you what's going to happen along the way.*

Abram's call came with a promise too. God said, "I will make of you a great nation, and I will bless you and make your name great, so that you will be a blessing. I will bless those who bless you, and him who dishonors you I will curse, and in you all the families of the earth shall be blessed" (vv. 2–3).

What if God came to you today and said the same thing? "You're going to be a huge blessing. I'm going to make you into a great nation. And everybody's going to be blessed through you." What would you think?

The honest answer I think a lot of people would give is, "I dunno. That's not what I envisioned for my life. Is the way going to be hard? What's it going to cost me? Are my friends going to come too?" And that's okay, because that was Abram's specific call, not yours or mine.

But let's get our minds around the bigger theme of that call to Abram. God was saying, "Here's a big promise. I'm going to impact a lot of people in a good way through you." That's a promise most of us would take. And notice that Abram's promise only came on the back side of God's calling to him. The call was to first leave what was comfortable. It was to step forward in faith into the unknown with God. Only then would the blessing come.

The Bible specifically notes that Abram was seventy-five years old when this all went down (v. 4). Seventy-five! Abram was no young man, and this blows up two myths: first, that a person needs to have life figured out when he or she is twenty, and second, that God doesn't give great callings to people when they're older and established in life.

God never wants anybody to check out, no matter how old or young. God is looking for people to take steps based not on age but on how we're gazing at his greatness. Up to the moment when we die at the end of our lives, everything else is fair game. God wants us to keep an open hand, to continually say to God, "I trust you to lead me." We need to get on the track that says, "I only live once. I'm never going to retire from God's plans for me." Our lives are always safest, not when we have a good paying job or a big retirement account or when we live in the suburbs with a white picket fence, but when our lives are firmly placed in the hands of God.

2. Dwell in the Land and Befriend Faithfulness

The second task when heading toward a comeback is practical. It's what we do while we're waiting. It's part of the comeback process. It happens on the road to a comeback, and it happens while a comeback is active and in progress.

While we're waiting and trusting in the Lord for the plans and purposes of our lives and saying, "God, I trust in you," the task for us to do is to dwell in the land and cultivate faithfulness. This implies that we don't see all the purposes of God fully unfolded yet. That's okay, because most of God's plans are unseen to us anyway. In this journey of faith, our confidence comes from God's character, what's been revealed about him in the Bible. And our confidence also comes in trusting that God is working even when we don't understand or see what's happening around us. Hebrews 11:1 says our faith doesn't rest on what's seen, but what's unseen.

I know that's hard for people to grab on to. Because they're saying, "Let me tell you what my reality looks like. My marriage just blew up. My family is under fire. I just lost my job. My best friend has cancer. I can't get free from this addiction that's keeping me down. Everything's going crazy in our world right now.

How can God possibly be orchestrating any grand and phenomenal plans in my life right now?"

I know it's difficult. But, yes, God is working even in the midst of whatever problem you're going through. He's working in both seen and unseen ways. He's working to put you on a path that you'll never regret, a path of extraordinary goodness that's a reflection of his character. In the meantime, your task is to dwell in the land and cultivate faithfulness. That means that today you have one major assignment: trust God for your future and cultivate faithfulness for whatever's in your hands at the moment.

None of us can cop out and say, "I don't know what God wants me to do, so I'm just going to check out." No, that's not God's purpose for you. He wants you to understand that there are no wasted moments. For his glory he uses everything that's happened, everything that's happening, and everything that will happen—past, present, and future.

When I was in college in Atlanta, I had several jobs. I worked for the Atlanta Hawks basketball team, the Atlanta Flames hockey team (yes, before they moved to Calgary), and the Centers for Disease Control and Prevention (CDC). My job at the CDC would be considered low-tech.

Of course, there wasn't a lot of high-tech going on back then. This was long before the Internet—I know that's hard to get our minds around today. The CDC maintained a huge library, and epidemiologists and doctors would visit the library and research whatever diseases they were treating. The library catalogued and stored innumerable bound journals, and doctors consulted them constantly. They'd fill out a request slip and tell me, "I want a copy of this article and this article and that article." And every academic medical journal article is about thirty-five pages long—minimum! I photocopied the requested articles and organized them so the requesting doctor could pick them up in a day or two. I was the copy guy. It wasn't glamorous work, but that's what I did. In some small way, however, I was changing the world. At least that's the way I saw it.

I can remember so many days when I'd come to work and find four carts stacked with journals with copy request slips protruding from them. I worked a four-hour shift each afternoon, and the photocopy room did not live up to any workplace standards. It was in the back of the library and under a stairwell. That room was as hot as an oven. There was no circulating air. The place stank with the smell of copier fluid. The ceiling slanted down, and I hit my head on it more times than I can remember. A boiler above the ceiling rattled and made lots of noise. You couldn't even get the carts inside the little room. They stayed outside and around a corner while I shuttled armfuls of journals back and forth. In that environment, I copied thousands of pages a day.

But here was my thinking. *I'm in this little room every day, and it's not like this is brain-intensive work. That means I have time to be with Jesus every day in this copy room. I can do my job and worship here while I do it.*

And I vowed to do that hourly wage job well. I made it my goal that no matter how many carts were waiting for me, I was going to do that photocopying to the best of my ability. I was working for Jesus and I was working with Jesus and I was talking to Jesus while I worked and he was talking with me. My photocopying was going to be the absolute finest it could be because it was being done for the glory of Jesus.

I did that job for a couple of years, and then it was time for me to move on to grad school. I loved hearing later that they needed to hire three people to do all the copy work I'd been doing, because the Jesus-loving machine of me was gone. I don't know what was happening in the minds and hearts of the employees who followed me, but I don't think they saw that job as the great opportunity I did to hang out with Jesus. They probably thought it was just a crummy job and hated every second of it.

The great thing about that job now, looking back, is that that photocopying job is intrinsically woven into the fabric of who I am today. My finished work was visible, but my working was not. But I wasn't unseen by God. I wasn't off his radar. I was in the proving grounds of character, and by God's grace I was dwelling in the land and cultivating faithfulness. Something deeply significant was happening in that moment, although it didn't feel significant at the time. A big part of God's process and plans for anyone who goes through God's proving grounds. That's where we don't see what's happening and where we don't see how it's all going to fit together and where it doesn't feel like any grand adventure anyone would write a book about. We just decide in our hearts and minds that we're going to be faithful.

Those are the moments where God says, *When you are faithful with little, then I know I can trust you with more.* But if we are fighting against the little things, then God won't lead us to anything bigger.

3. Delight Yourself in the Lord, and He Will Give You the Desires of Your Heart

Your third step is to delight in God. When we do, God gives us something in return: the desires of our heart.

It's a promise God makes, yet we've got to notice the sequence of how this verse is laid out. The delighting comes first.

The fulfillment of our desires happens second. Whenever that sequence is understood and lived out, we don't need to worry about what our desires may be, because we delight in God first and then our desires will follow suit. If we will make Jesus our first priority, our desires morph and change over time as God shapes them.

I wanted to be a doctor when I was little, then a politician when I was in high school. That was the big desire of my heart back then. Then I went to college to play tennis, thinking that was my future, but none of those things were the path for me. Then God called me into ministry. I eventually became a communications major and then ended up at seminary. When I first got to seminary, I thought about all the different boxes I could check for ministry calling: pastor, youth pastor, associate pastor, evangelist, minister of education, missionary. I didn't think I fit into any of those boxes. I couldn't figure out my desires, because my desires didn't fit into what looked normal to other people.

What's great now is that I know that Jesus trumps our desires. Jesus opens up a story for us that fulfills (and exceeds) our heart's desire if we delight in him. Jesus doesn't cram us into preset molds; he molds us for God-birthed purposes.

4. Commit Your Way to the Lord; Trust in Him, and He Will Act

Jesus invites us to commit our ways to him. That's the fourth task: trust in him. And it comes with a promise: He. Will. Act.

Step by step, God will make our comeback happen. He will bring about what he wants in our lives. He will unfold his plan in his time and his way. And it will be like nothing we could dream up ourselves. For year after year we had stayed with the students at Baylor and been faithful to that calling. Now God was about to do something beyond our imagination.

Several confusing months passed after we moved back to Atlanta. We were frustrated, and our purpose for moving was still cloudy.

Then, in July 1995, I went to speak at a conference in Dallas. On the plane I was reading a magazine, and I remember specifically looking at an advertisement for a new convention center in Daytona Beach, Florida, of all places, and—this is hard to fully explain—but I just went away for a while, and I saw something I had never seen before.

Suddenly, and unexpectedly, I saw a vision that almost stopped my heart.

In front of me were more college students than I'd ever seen before. It was a sea of college students, as far as the eye could see. They were all on their knees, and they were all praying for their generation. They were worshiping God and calling out in prayer. They were praising God and asking him for a great spiritual awakening in their time.

I don't know how long the vision lasted, but when it was over, I was looking at that advertisement in the magazine again.

When I came back to my seat on the plane, I could hardly breathe. I just sat there. Stunned.

Soon I knew that this was what Shelley and I were going to do. I didn't know what it all meant or how we were going to get there. I certainly didn't have the phrase *Passion Conferences* in mind. But I knew that this was the direction God was leading Shelley and me to go. The vision was such a powerful thing to me that I didn't tell Shelley about it for two weeks. The vision wasn't simply an impression on my heart. It was a take-your-breath-away kind of vision. One that was real.

When Shelley and I started talking about it, she didn't think I was crazy. She amazingly said, "Okay, that's what we'll do." Then I went to two spiritual leaders—who were friends of mine and had given their lives for college students—and asked, "What would you think of a gathering of college students unlike anything we've seen in our lifetime—a gathering where tens of thousands of students would come together for a solemn assemby and pray for spiritual awakening." The only expectation I had was that these leaders might pray about the idea.

Both guys said, "Wow, it's so amazing that you'd say that. Because I've been thinking and praying about the exact same thing."

There was an immediate resonance with the idea as we talked to more people—it wasn't just "Louie's idea." I didn't need to convince or persuade anybody of anything. I went to the board of directors of our former ministry at Baylor—they were all wondering what we were going to do—and I shared what God had put on my heart. After a lot of prayer and seeking the face of God, they said, "Yes, this is it."

It took several months for us to name it Passion. It took more months after that before we figured out where to begin and started planning a conference to be called Passion 1997 in Austin, Texas. Eventually, we held that first conference. Two thousand students gathered for four days of worship, teaching, and prayer rooted in the confession, "Your name and renown are the desire of our souls." In 1998, Passion doubled to five thousand, and in 1999, eleven thousand jammed the Fort Worth

Convention Arena. All this happened mostly through word of mouth. All of it was Jesus uniting his people.

When a Plan Comes Together

Then, on May 20, 2000, in Memphis, Tennessee, we saw that initial vision partially come to life, that same picture I saw while on the plane. Only this time, it wasn't a vision. There was a sea of college students, forty thousand strong, spread out far and wide. They had gathered from every state in the US, and around the world, and were kneeling on a hillside, praying for spiritual awakening in their generation. It was a holy day, one of the most holy moments of my life. After OneDay 2000, and after we picked our hearts up off the floor, I thought, *Well, that's that. Mission accomplished. That was the vision.* But God said, *No, that's only part of the story.* And we're still on that Passion journey today.

So back to my father's death. Fast-forward to New Year's Eve 2012 and the Georgia Dome in Atlanta. The next day, January 1, we were going to begin four days of Passion 2013, the largest conference for college students we'd ever done before. But first, a college football bowl was going to take place in the Dome on New Year's night. I was asked to give the invocation for that game (yes, there is still a collegiate bowl game that begins with prayer), so I walked onto the field and prayed for the game and all who were taking part. When it ended, the bowl game moved out and we got ready to move in and start our event the next day. Amazingly, our team loaded in one of the largest events that has ever been set up in the Georgia Dome in less than twenty-four hours. Three hundred thousand pounds of equipment and staging.

The field was turned over to us around 1 a.m., and we started our event at 7 p.m. the next night. Some sixty thousand college students filled the stadium to worship Jesus. The event was in the round, so our stage was placed in the middle of the field on the fifty yard line. As I walked up to speak in that opening session, all I could think about was what was under my feet. No, not the stage itself, but what was underneath it. Though covered by the material used to protect the surface of the field, I knew the sponsor's logo from the bowl game was still painted on that very spot. They hadn't had time to wash it away in the quick turnaround. So, crazily, under my feet and directly under our stage for our entire conference was the Chick-fil-A logo the size of your living room. What's the significance, you ask?

Well, in 1964, my dad—as a freelance graphic designer—created the Chick-fil-A logo. For the next four days, at the largest Passion gathering to date, I was going to literally stand and lead on top of a logo created by my dad.

Leading in the Georgia Dome on top of that logo was as if God was reminding me, *I don't often explain everything fully in this life, but, I realize in some ways the timing of your father's death and your move to Atlanta has never made sense to you. You need to know that, through your father's death, you and Shelley were put into a position of vulnerability . . . a time when I loosened all of the soil of your lives and shifted everything dear to you. I did all that to place you in a window of life where I could create the vision for Passion Conferences and touch the lives of all these people. And eighteen years after your father's death, I have you standing at your biggest event to date on top of the logo created by your dad. Louie, I'm a sovereign God, and I'm orchestrating the events of this world. I'm running everything. I'm in charge of it all. I've got a purpose and a plan, and nothing gets lost in my economy. Nothing is wasted. No tear, no sorrow, no depression, no death—nothing is wasted when it comes to my purposes. I'm a good God and your Father, and I'm weaving everything into a beautiful plan for all of eternity.*

It's not easy for me to transfer through words on a page just how much my heart—all of our hearts—hurt during those seven years between the onset of my dad's illness and his death. But without really knowing how, instinctively we were staying put in Texas, trusting that God was bigger than our situation, being faithful with what was in our hands right then, and believing that whatever God's plans were, they were for good and not evil.

Now we were standing in a vista that filled us with humility and awe.

I don't believe my dad had to become disabled, suffer, and die for Passion to happen. But this moment was a confirmation for me that God paints on a canvas bigger than I can imagine. And that bolstered my faith in his unassailable plans.

I guess we could have gone a more normal, direct, and less challenging route. But through the wilderness of suffering and death, God prepared us for what was to come.

How about you? Have you found yourself in a detour? A delay? A side story that looks like it's taking you further from your ambition, not toward it?

A comeback might not start out as you plan or think. But if you just wait, God will show you how he's weaving all the pieces of the story together for a greater good. It's always tempting to question whether God is part of the events of your life, particularly when you can't figure it all out. But he's definitely there.

Sometimes you need to wait all the way to heaven, and he'll show you only then.

If you are in that season of wandering or waiting, let me encourage you that God is still at work. God has not forgotten you. You are still a part of his great plan. Your comeback will probably look different than you have imagined it, and that's okay. Wait and believe. God is the God of the comeback, and God is creating a comeback especially for you. You cannot control the outcomes, but you can determine how you will order your steps around his Word. Breathe out all the stress, because these are your only tasks today:

1. Trust in the Lord, and do good.
2. Dwell in the land and befriend faithfulness.
3. Delight yourself in the Lord, and he will give you the desires of your heart.
4. Commit your way to the Lord; trust in him, and he will act.

ELEVEN

TO THE OTHER SIDE OF EMPTY

In the late summer of 1981, I sat and waited in the lobby of the dean of life sciences at Georgia State University. My main mission seemed impossible: I desperately needed to get back into school.

The previous spring, for a lot of reasons I felt I could justify back then, I'd ended up receiving a nice letter from the people at George State kindly inviting me to take two quarters off. I'd flunked out of college. My grades were in the tank. I rarely went to classes. I think my GPA was below 1.0. I was getting grades I didn't previously know existed (like WF—withdrew failing). Oddly, during my *hiatus* from GSU, I took a shot at rehabilitating things at a nearby junior college (now Kennesaw State University). I flunked out of there as well. Impressive. When I say I flunked out, I'm not saying I went to classes, applied myself, did my best, and couldn't cut it. Let's just say I was completely under-motivated. Uninterested. For sure, I went *toward* class most days. I just didn't actually make it *to* class. I liked being downtown on campus. I loved hanging out with my friends. I loved playing Ping-Pong and pool and going to the student life center and having Blimpie's subs for lunch. I was working as a part-time youth pastor and loving it, and that job was a lot of what I used as an excuse. I was serving Jesus, and I thought I didn't have time for the mundane rigors of school.

Early that morning in late summer 1981, before I ended up waiting in the dean's lobby, I was driving up I-75, heading toward the community college I was flunking out of. I was near the Windy Hill Road exit, and I sensed God impressing something on my heart. *So, Louie, you want to be a preacher someday, right?*

And I did. In spite of my shortcomings, I felt called to ministry and had for a year or so. I knew beyond any shadow of a doubt, God wanted me to leverage my life to tell people about Jesus and preach his Word. I was captivated, compelled, and decided.

God impressed, *So, someday you'll need to go to seminary. Correct?*

Yep, I thought. *Can't wait. I want to be equipped in the best way possible.*

Then you know you need to have an undergraduate degree in order to go to seminary, right? The point was crystal clear.

Hello.

Something clicked inside my head that had not happened in my short and illustrious collegiate career. That's how short-sighted I'd been. My mom had been begging me to go to class. All my friends were earning good grades and moving on. They knew I was crashing out of everything, and they'd said things from time to time. Little nudges here and there.

Yet, in that instant, my perspective completely shifted.

Right away, I exited the expressway, turned my car around, and drove straight to Georgia State. It was past the registration date for the fall by about four days and classes had already started. I went straight to the dean's office, gave the assistant a brief overview of my situation, and asked if I could see him. It was midmorning. She said no, not today.

Hmmm.

"Here's what I'm going to do," I said. "I'm going to sit right here on this sofa the rest of the day. If he's got a five-minute window anytime today, I'll be here."

So I sat down.

I waited and waited and waited. I waited about three hours, the nice lady at the desk peering over inquisitively every few minutes or so. Finally, she said, "You've got five minutes," and motioned her head toward the dean's door.

I was praying with all the faith I had when I walked through the door.

The dean told me to sit down and asked my name and student ID number. I told him and then held my breath as I watched him typing into his computer. I knew he had pulled up my transcript, because his eyes grew wide and he muttered, "Wow. I'm not sure I've seen too many like this."

I thought it might be a good idea if I spoke first. "I know I've been a horrible student. It's not because I'm not smart. I haven't tried at all. I've been totally aimless. An idiot. But I need to go to grad school because I'm supposed to be a pastor, and I need to get back in school and get my undergraduate degree. I will change. I will work hard, I promise. Please, sir, I need to get back into school and on the track of getting my degree."

He looked carefully at me but didn't say anything more. He picked up his phone and made a call. I don't know what kind of strings he pulled or what kind of miracle God worked, but I registered at Georgia State that afternoon and started classes the next day.

I'd truly changed. I knew I needed to make up for lost time. A normal load at Georgia State back then was fifteen hours. Over the next four quarters (this was before GSU switched to semesters) I took twenty-plus-hour loads, and in my final summer quarter I took thirty-five hours. In those four quarters, I ended up doing two years of college work and graduated in time to load my car and head to Fort Worth for seminary.

That was a big comeback in my life. I went from an under-motivated college kid who'd been kicked out of school for his horrible grades to a highly motivated college kid who was serious about his studies and determined to succeed.

I'm sharing this story with you for a couple of reasons. One, it's important for you to know I haven't spent my whole life on big stages speaking to thousands of people. And, not that you would probably think otherwise, but to make sure you understand I'm a struggler like you. In fact, your very struggle right now may be exactly like mine in that season of my life. You have a God-sized dream, a love for Jesus, and can't be bothered by mundane things like going to class and finishing school. I can't speak for you, but I know for me, Jesus wasn't being honored by me being a careless and wasteful student. Especially since he had given me the capacity to do more. It wasn't just my grades that were at stake. His reputation was at stake. A Jesus-following student who does less than their best communicates something to their teachers and advisors about their faith. I was communicating exactly the *wrong* thing. And, worse, I was blaming my laziness on my godliness, and that's a joke.

Also—and this one's a far bigger reason—I'm sharing this with you because I want to tell you that the dream and possibility of my life didn't end that day while I was waiting for the dean on the sofa outside his office. Failing school was a part of my life, but in the greater scope of things, it's a far less significant part of my life. And it wasn't the end of my story.

Yes, there was a part of my life where I failed, and there was a zero moment, a place where I had hit empty and was desperate for a turnaround—when I sat waiting on the dean's sofa not knowing what was going to happen next. But worst-case, I would wait another quarter, reenter GSU, and just delay my seminary schedule. I say this because if you are at that *zero moment* you might be thinking this is the end. But it's not.

What's Most Important?

Getting your mind around that is important because when we talk about the comeback process, it may seem like we focus on the failure in a person's life a lot—the part that needs to be flipped around or made new again. Sure, that's important, to hit that zero moment where you definitely know you can't continue in the direction you're heading. You long for a comeback. You're eager for a fresh start.

Yet it's vital to note that the empty (or below empty, if you feel that's where you are) is never what's most important in the process. What's on the *other* side of empty is what we want to focus on, because the true purpose for which God has created you is on the other side of empty. That's what you want. That's what you're heading toward. New life. The important part of your life is not your failings, even if you fail your entire life and have a comeback one hour before you die. That one hour of living in God's true purpose for you is more important than everything that went before it.

We have so many voices in our heads every day telling us who we need to be . . . or who we are. And some of those voices are adding up that you are a failure for one reason or another. Or, like me, you may have *actually* failed.

But that's not who we truly are.

Who we truly are is who God created us to be. That's what's most important. Our true identity is seen in light of God. He determines the destiny of our life. My prayer for you as you read this book is that God's Word and his voice will break into your heart and you'll embrace and believe what God says about who you truly are. That's the beauty of a comeback. You start a process thinking one way about yourself, and then God opens your eyes and you begin a whole new journey with God.

We can clearly see this in the life of the apostle Paul, whose name was originally Saul. Paul was succeeding in the world's eyes (at least the religious and intellectual world of his day). But he was on the complete opposite page from Jesus. He needed a comeback and he might not have even known it. But in an instant, everything changed. In fact, Paul's life can be summarized in two short verses:

> Paul, an apostle of Christ Jesus by the will of God,
>
> To the saints who are in Ephesus, and are faithful in Christ Jesus:
>
> Grace to you and peace from God our Father and the Lord Jesus Christ. (Ephesians 1:1–2)

Those two verses look pretty simple, don't they? If you were to preach on those two verses, you probably wouldn't get too many people shouting back at you! At first glance, the opening of the letter to the Ephesians appears to be a simple greeting. But I have to tell you, the opening salutation of anything in the Word of God is full of power, and these two verses unpack the heartbeat of Paul's new life and what God is saying in the book of Ephesians as a whole.

Let's look at four huge takeaways from these two verses. These takeaways relate to Paul's life as well as ours.

1. God Has the Power to Change Our Name and Our Destiny

I can't get too far into Ephesians without stopping at the first word: Paul. That single word is a picture of the gospel. He's saying, "This is who I am. My name is Paul, and I'm an apostle, an ambassador of Jesus Christ. I'm on a mission for Jesus by the will of God, and I'm writing to you and letting you know who's writing—Paul." The reason that one word is so important is because, right out of the gate, we know that God has the power to change our name and our destiny.

The backstory here is that after Jesus was resurrected and had ascended into heaven and the new church was born, not everybody was happy with that, particularly some of the Jewish leaders. They tried as hard as they could to squash what they considered to be a heretical religious movement. One leader who tried hard to stamp out the early faith in Jesus Christ was a man named Saul of Tarsus.

The name Saul means "small" or "diminutive," so we know that he wasn't a giant, broad-shouldered kind of guy. He was small in stature and possibly had a physical infirmity, a weakness that caused him to seem even smaller. So we've got a little bitty guy, but he's brilliant.

We know from another letter that he was born into a good Jewish family. And even though he was Jewish, he was a Roman citizen and was educated in the best schools. So he was smart and bright and highly educated in the Jewish religious system. He became a leader and was zealous for the religious system he was raised in. He, too, was looking for a messiah; it's just he was convinced Jesus *wasn't* the one. He developed a venomous hatred toward the resurrection story of Jesus, and he was given authority to do whatever was necessary to stop it. He could throw people in prison. He could ransack people's homes. He even had the authority to kill people if that was required to silence the Christians. And he did all of these things.

One day Saul was headed toward the town of Damascus, and he was excited to get there because he knew Christians were active there, and Saul wanted to do his job. But on the way, Saul met Jesus Christ in a vision. The radiance of Jesus in the vision was so powerful that it knocked Saul to the ground and physically blinded him. Jesus said, "Saul, Saul, why are you persecuting me?" (Acts 9:4).

The vision completely shut Saul down. For several days afterward, he couldn't see. Then God sent a representative to Saul saying, "This has happened for this reason: God has chosen to take you out of the business of crushing the gospel and into the business of spreading the gospel. He's chosen to take you out of being a hater of the faith to being a follower of Jesus. You've got a whole new mission, friend. You're going to be an ambassador for Jesus Christ." Saul's eyes were opened, and his name was changed to Paul.

That's why that one little word at the start of Ephesians is so powerful. That's the power of the gospel right there. Saul was changed to Paul. A dreadful past was changed to an amazing hope-filled future. God can do this for us today. He can change our names and our destiny. That means we're not what we were. Saul was a self-righteous, murderous zealot, and he became a proclaimer of the peace and grace found in Jesus.

Paul's past wasn't something to be celebrated, but it was something God would use. Imagine the moment when he entered a Christian's home after he met Jesus. The word on the street was this guy killed Jesus-people. Is it true? Has he changed? Is he one of us? Should we be afraid?

Yet, how amazing to then experience the transforming power of God's forgiveness because of the Jesus that is now in this man's eyes. In that moment, you would believe that there was hope for a comeback for anyone, anywhere, anytime.

It doesn't matter what you've done and where you've been. It doesn't matter what's been said about you. You may have been the worst of the worst. You may have hated Jesus. Yet, through the power of his Word, God wants to redefine who you are. He can literally turn your world around. He did so with Saul. He can do it for you. Who knows? Maybe you're going to be the one who births faith in a whole generation of people. Maybe you thought you'd lost your shot to be a part of what God's doing. But God's saying, *Oh, no, you haven't. You're going to have such a big role in my future plans for my people, it's going to blow your mind. I'm the one who changed Saul to Paul. I change people's names. I change people's destiny. And I can do that in your life as well.*

2. Our Circumstances Don't Inhibit God from Fulfilling His Plans and Purposes

Before a comeback arrives, it's easy to feel stuck in our circumstances. We think we're not going anywhere. We're always going to remain in the position we are now. But here's a good reminder. When Paul started writing to the Ephesians, he was actually stuck in jail with chains on his wrists.

The backstory here is that years after Saul's name was changed to Paul, he left Jerusalem and planted churches around the Mediterranean world, one of which was in the important port city of Ephesus. Hundreds of thousands of people lived there, and it was a bustling, influential place. Paul stayed for two years in Ephesus and poured his life out for the people there. He raised people up in truth, preached the Word of God, proclaimed the story of the resurrection of Jesus, and worked a second job as a tentmaker to help raise up a little church that could be a beacon of light in the city.

He left Ephesus and returned to Jerusalem. But when he arrived, he learned that the religious leaders in Jerusalem wanted to take him out. So Paul slipped away to the port city of Caesarea, where he stayed for a while until the religious leaders tracked him down. But this time, instead of running, Paul pulled out his citizenship papers and said, "If I'm going to be arrested, I've got a right to be tried by the leaders in Rome. Take me there." So the religious leaders had no choice but to put him on a boat and ship him to Rome, just as God said would happen. You see, Paul was going to take the gospel to the rulers of all the known world.

Paul lived under house arrest in Rome for two years. The emperor at the time was Nero, who became famous for his persecution of Christians. Nero was so demented that he actually set Christians on fire and used them as living torches for his gardens at night.

It's from that crazy, dangerous environment that Paul was moved by the Holy Spirit to write to the Ephesians. Note how

Paul *doesn't* begin the letter. He could have started out by talking about how he wanted to do something great to encourage the people in Ephesus, but he's sorry, he can't, because he's in prison, and he's miserable there.

Nope. He doesn't do that. Instead, Paul launched straight into the letter with a huge encouragement. It's as if he's saying, "Even when you're under house arrest, the Holy Spirit can still flood through your life in powerful ways. I might be in chains, but my circumstances can't limit God from doing what God wants to do through my life. You may be stuck in your circumstances, but you are still free to be used by the Spirit of God to do whatever it is that God wants to do in and through your life."

That's a big takeaway for us in this passage, because some of us have narrowly defined who we are based on our lousy circumstances. And God reminds us that he is far greater than any circumstances. Whatever circumstances you find yourself in today, those circumstances will never hinder God from doing what he wants to do in your life.

3. God Always Starts with Who We Are, Not What We Do

I love this third takeaway. In the second part of verse 1, Paul identifies himself and his readers as "an apostle of Christ by the will of God, to the saints who are in Ephesus, and are faithful in Christ Jesus."

I love that word *saints*. It's a word we don't use much to describe ourselves, but that's how Paul described the believers in Ephesus. They were ordinary people, but because they were connected to Jesus, everything had changed. Sometimes that word is translated as "holy ones," and that's powerful too. Yet, I still love the word *saints* because it's a strong identity word, especially for people who have called themselves sinners all their lives. What it implies at the beginning of this letter is that God starts with who we are before he talks about what we do.

That's the opposite of religion. Religion starts with what you do and works its way toward what you might become. Maybe you've been caught up in that, the thought that if you do enough good things and change how you behave, then maybe you can become the person God wants you to be.

God doesn't work like that. God starts with an act of faith in which we join our lives to Jesus. Something happens inside of us. We become brand-new creatures in Jesus Christ. God starts with who we've become, and then he works his way to how we live. God wants our identity to shape how we live, not the other way around.

And I love the positive slant that's shown in that first verse. Paul could have called the Ephesians any number of things. He could have called them sinners saved by grace, which would have been a true designation. But here's the problem with that: if you go around thinking of yourself first and foremost as a sinner saved by grace, then it becomes highly likely that you'll see yourself primarily as a sinner first and saved by grace second. And when you go around calling yourself a sinner, you're much more likely to act like a sinner, even if you're saved by grace. If you think of yourself primarily as a sinner, you're going to act like a sinner.

Paul deliberately used the word *saints*. And he wrote to *regular people*. Do you see the incredible power of what he was doing? Paul wasn't writing to the statues of dead people. He wasn't writing to a woman who spent all of her life working in the slums of Calcutta. He wasn't writing to people who had performed a certain number of miracles. He was writing to little kids, teenagers, moms and dads, grandmas and grandpas. He was writing to anyone who'd put their faith in Jesus Christ, and he was calling them saints.

He was calling *us* saints. We need to get that straight before we go much further because it means that I'm a miracle and so are you. My life and destiny have been changed, and so have yours. My name's been changed, and your name's been changed too. We are not sinners; we are saints.

The literal translation of this word means that we are the holy ones of God because of our faith in Christ Jesus. We don't get to be holy simply because we like the idea of being holy. We get to be holy because we have put our faith in Christ. Holiness is handed to us by Jesus; he puts his holiness in and on us. Jesus can do this because he came to earth, died for the sins of the world, was raised by the power of God, and is giving us life because we trust in him. We are born again to brand-new life. This is the divine exchange—the innocent (Jesus) for the guilty (you and me); his righteousness transferred into our account forever. Our new identity is that we are the holy ones made holy in Christ by God through grace by faith. We are now the saints of God in the world.

Why doesn't Paul write to the sinners saved by grace? Because the intended outcome of this letter isn't about more sinning; the intended outcome of this letter is about more holy living. And to get more holy living, God reminds us of who we are. We're holy people already in Jesus Christ. When we're reminded of our true identity, we can head toward holy living. We can still sin, for sure. But we aren't sinners anymore at our core. We're saints. Hello! Grasp this radical idea with everything you've got! We are saints of God in Christ, holy ones of God.

4. The Way of Jesus Is the Way of Grace and Peace

The second verse reads, "Grace to you and peace from God our Father and the Lord Jesus Christ." That's more than a simple salutation. When we know our new identity in Christ it affects how we live. We're marked by grace, and that means less striving and more trusting in God's power to do what only God can do. Our lives will become marked by peace. That means less fighting, less warring, less contention, less going to bed angry, less anger between us and the people around us, and more peacefulness.

Everybody wants grace and peace. It's possible because we're now joined to Jesus. Grace and peace are reflective of our new position in Christ. When we put our faith in Jesus, we don't join an organization. We join with Jesus. Our goal isn't to get inside a building. Our goal is to join with the person of Christ. And when we put our faith in Christ, our lives and stories and pasts and presents and futures are inseparably joined together with Jesus' life and story and past and present and future. Our abilities are joined to his abilities. Our dreams are joined to his dreams. Our destiny is joined to his destiny.

That means that becoming a Christ-follower involves more than simply saying we believe in something. We are joined to someone! We literally join our lives to his. Have you ever used the phrase *We're in*? For example, when you're in business and you get a call from a prospective customer or partner and he agrees to join you, and he says, "We're in." Or in school, one of your friends invites you to go somewhere, and you say, "Okay, I'm in." It means that you have been joined to the environment, the circumstance, the people, the relationships. You've joined to access an opportunity you've been hoping for.

The same is true when you come to faith in Jesus Christ. You're in. You're in the faith, in the family, in the destiny. You have new opportunities and new possibilities because your life has been joined to Jesus. In Ephesians, the phrase "in Christ" is used ten times in the first fourteen verses. That is,

You're blessed in Christ.

You're redeemed in Christ.

You have forgiveness of sins in Christ.

You were chosen in Christ to be holy and blameless.

You have every spiritual blessing in Christ.

You were included in Christ.

You've been made aware of the plans of God in Christ.

In Christ you've been sealed with the Holy Spirit.

In Christ you've been loved.

In Christ is where the hope comes.

This isn't based on how we feel on any given day or emotion. It is a reality from the instant we come to life by faith in Christ. It's like when your favorite player is traded from your city to another. That very moment the deal is executed, the player is now fully a member of another team, whether they feel like it or not. For them to wear the old uniform doesn't make sense anymore. Now it's a new process of adjusting to their new identity.

In a more powerful way, our salvation is not only about a belief about Jesus. It's about actually taking up residence *in* Jesus. When that happens, our identities change. We move away from our old selves and toward the identity of Christ in us, the hope of glory. Our new identity is that we have Christ living in us. We are supernaturally joined with Jesus. We are intertwined into a new identity. We have moved from death to life. From *me* to *Jesus*. From sinners to saints. You know what that means? It means that if Jesus died, I died. It means that if Jesus rose, I rose. If Jesus lives, I live. If Jesus wins, I win. If Jesus can, I can. If Jesus won't, I won't. If Jesus would, I would. If Jesus says to rise above it, I rise above it. If Jesus says that this is the way, I walk in it. If Jesus says that these are the people I want to serve and love, I serve and love these people. If Jesus says that these are the ways I want to spend my resources, then I spend my resources in these ways.

It's Jesus in me, me in Jesus. We're inseparably linked by grace through faith.

Where the Hope Comes

What happened to Paul after he started living for Christ? It wasn't all easy for Paul, and that's an important part of realizing what can be involved in a comeback. Difficulties still happen. In Paul's case, a lot of difficulties came into his life. In 2 Corinthians 11:16–33, Paul lists them. He needed to work hard. He was imprisoned. He was beaten with rods and lashed with whips and pelted with stones. He encountered dangers while traveling. Three times he was shipwrecked and spent a day and night in the open sea. A lot of people didn't like him much. He sometimes went without sleep. He knew what it meant to be hungry and thirsty. He was continually burdened for the people he helped.

I say this carefully, but it's true: our comeback stories may involve some of those difficulties too. That's the paradox of a comeback. We long for a comeback. We need a comeback. And much good comes in a comeback. But difficulties can still be involved in the comeback process.

Paul put his difficulties into perspective:

If I must boast, I will boast of the things that show my weakness.

[God] said to me, "My grace is sufficient for you, for my power is made perfect in weakness." Therefore I will boast all the more gladly about my weaknesses, so that the power of Christ may rest upon me. For the sake of Christ, then, I am content with weaknesses, insults, hardships, persecutions, and calamities. For when I am weak, then I am strong. (2 Corinthians 11:30, 12:9–10)

Our comebacks may involve difficulty. Our comebacks will almost always look different from what we expect, and yet our comebacks will always be better. Why? Because God writes the story of our comebacks, and God is always good and glorious. In Paul's case, he went on to write much of the New Testament. He was a pillar of the early church. He testified about Jesus before the world's greatest leaders. He saw any number of miracles firsthand. In Jesus' name, Paul helped change countless lives for better. Paul lived a vastly significant life.

And since Paul was "in Christ," it meant his empty, zero moment was long behind him. His past was forgotten. Paul became a new being who was dead to his old self and alive to his new self. His new self was given a future and a hope because of Christ. The vast majority of the New Testament doesn't tell us about who the old Saul was. But it contains story after story about the new life Paul had in Jesus. Paul went on to live for Jesus and hold on to hope in Jesus and to spread the news of Jesus. Paul spread light in the darkness because of Jesus, and Paul's story wasn't even about Paul anymore; it was about living for the glory of Jesus.

God had a future and a hope for Paul. Jesus changed Paul's name from Saul, and Jesus gave a new destiny to this man who was once such a God-hater. That's the beauty of the comeback that Paul had. The story of Saul was rewritten.

And that can be your comeback story too. The most important part of your story is not where you've been or what you've done. It's not that you flunked out of university or blew it or procrastinated or hit bottom or failed in your marriage or ruined your career or wrecked your parents' car. The most important part of your story is that by faith you are in Christ and Christ is now in you.

That means you are no longer stuck. You're not stuck in your circumstances, and you're not stuck with your failings or shortcomings. By faith you are now in Christ. You've made the leap. Your identity is changed. You have a new position in Christ.

This is how Paul expressed this in words:

In him you also, when you heard the word of truth, the gospel of your salvation, and believed in him, were sealed with the promised Holy Spirit. (Ephesians 1:13)

That means that when you believed, the Holy Spirit came rushing in and everything changed inside. It means right now you have the power to turn the car around. You are united with Jesus, and you have a brand-new answer to the question of your identity. Everything's changed in your comeback. You are in Christ right now and forever. That's who you truly are.

TWELVE

THE ULTIMATE COMEBACK

People often wonder: *Why do Christians think their way is the best way to believe? How come Jesus is the answer? What about every other faith leader? Aren't their religions just as good?*

It's a valid question, one that indicates a person is doing some soul-searching and wants to discover the truth. Eventually, I hope to lead them to the crux of our faith, the resurrection of Jesus from the dead.

This single event defines our hope and sets our faith apart from every other religious point of view. Our teacher is not dead. Our leader is not in the grave. Jesus is alive and on this our future rests.

The resurrection of Jesus is the pillar of the Christian faith. If we don't have this truth, then we are just another religion, with leaders who head a movement and maybe teach a few good things and attract a lot of followers. But when those leaders die, they stay dead.

To get up out of your coffin and smile at the folks gathered for your funeral, that's the ultimate comeback. Or—switching to first-century cultural patterns—to walk out of a tomb, living and breathing, smiling and holding out your hands to friends so they can check your scars to make sure it's really you, looking not at all pale and sickly but better than the best version of yourself that there's ever been, that's the ultimate comeback.

Think about it. A human body is lying there dead—graveclothes wrapped around the corpse, embalming done, stone rolled across the entry and sealed—on a stone bench. Suddenly blood begins to course through the veins again, and the heart begins to beat, and the cells start working again. The body takes a breath, stretches, stands up, comes out, walks around for everyone to see. And this body has lost any capacity to die again.

You see, all our comebacks are swallowed up by this ultimate comeback. Because Jesus is alive again, we can come back from anything the world throws at us:

- The deepest kind of sin
- The devastation of crumbling relationships
- The rejection of job loss and failure
- The general disappointment of life
- The pain of bereavement
- The hammer of betrayal
- Whatever, you name it

Jesus' ultimate comeback trumps all our comebacks, but it also makes it possible in a general sense for us to come back from anything, from anywhere, at any time. The secret is in how Jesus' resurrection life infuses our ordinary lives with the same kind of power.

In the classic resurrection passage, 1 Corinthians 15, the apostle Paul described the shape we'd all be in if Jesus had merely died and not come back—if he hadn't had that ultimate comeback from the tomb, never to die again.

What If Jesus Had Stayed Dead?

Some people questioned whether there was such a thing as the resurrection of the dead, any dead, and that's who Paul addressed here. They scoffed at the very idea of resurrection and patronized those who believed it, tending to dismiss them with a pat on the head and a roll of their eyes. These skeptics thought the sophisticated thing was to plow through life without answers and tell yourself you should be content without knowing anything for sure. Certainly, you had to be content without believing in such wild things as resurrection. They figured that only one thing was certain, and everybody knew that one thing: dead things stayed dead.

But Paul noted the pointlessness of life without an afterlife, the despair of rejecting the possibility of resurrection. It would mean there was no resurrection even for Jesus, that he stayed dead in the tomb. If he did, the whole thing Jesus was trying to accomplish comes crashing down. Paul wrote:

If there is no resurrection of the dead, then not even Christ has been raised. And if Christ has not been raised, then our preaching is in vain and your faith is in vain. We are even found to be misrepresenting God, because we testified about God that he raised Christ, whom he did not raise if it is true that the dead are not raised. For if the dead are not raised, not even Christ has been raised. And if Christ has not been raised, your faith is futile and you are still in your sins. Then those also who have fallen asleep in Christ have perished. If in Christ we have hope in this life only, we are of all people most to be pitied. (1 Corinthians 15:13–19)

Did you catch the hypothetical in this passage? Paul asked, "Let's just suppose Christ didn't rise from the dead. If that's the case, then our preaching might as well stop right now, and our faith, well, that's just plain silly and useless. You can't have a Christianity with a dead Jesus. It just goes nowhere. And you have to feel sorry for people who follow that sort of thing."

Paul said that if Jesus wasn't resurrected, there's nothing worth preaching about, Christianity is an empty faith with all the stuffing completely knocked out. Those who preach it are liars of the worst kind, and those who believe it are to be pitied.

The key phrase is "if Christ has not been raised . . . you are still in your sins." You see, the resurrection is God's great stamp of approval on the finished work of Christ on the cross, that what Jesus did there was good enough to permanently cancel our sin penalty. Let's dig into that a little.

Paul wrote, "[God] made him to be sin who knew no sin, so that in him we might become the righteousness of God" (2 Corinthians 5:21). That means that Christ accepted the sin of the world on the cross. When he died, it was a total, ultimate death.

We need to understand that the Bible refers to more than one kind of death, but they all involve separation:

- **Physical death** is the separation of the body from the spirit.
- **Spiritual death** is the separation of a person's spirit from God.
- **Eternal death** is spiritual death continued forever.

Jesus died physically on the cross, but he also died spiritually when the fellowship relationship between the Father and the Son was broken. Jesus announced that break as he hung from the cross and took on hell from the cross, saying, "My God, my God, why have you forsaken me?" (Mark 15:34). Then he declared, "It is finished" (John 19:30), meaning that the great work of redemption was finished, the sin of the entire world was paid for—past, present, and future.

But questions remain: How do we really know that the work of Christ on the cross was good enough? How can we have total confidence that the job was really finished? The answer is Christ's resurrection. Here's how Paul laid it out:

> [Christ] was delivered up for our trespasses and raised for our justification. (Romans 4:25)

The resurrection of Jesus Christ is the great display of the Father's power, as Paul said: "[That] is the immeasurable greatness of his power toward us who believe, according to the working of his great might that he worked in Christ when he raised him from the dead" (Ephesians 1:19–20).

That same power is available to us to live out our lives. We really don't ever need to be defeated, we don't need to be only half victorious. We can be complete winners in the best sense, namely, in the realm of the Spirit. The reason is that God has a huge vault of resurrection power, and we can write checks against it whenever we want. The resurrection is the great pivot on which the Christian faith balances, and it's the energy that fuels abundant life for a believer.

Did you get that? The resurrection power of almighty God

that brought Jesus up from the grip of death and hell is *living in you!*

We need to take hold of this. We need to be sure that we understand how important the resurrection of Jesus Christ is to us personally. It's the complete game changer. First, it guarantees that we can be freed from the need to pay for our own sins, and second, it makes power available to us to live our lives in victory.

Without the resurrection, we've got nothing.

Facts Speak for Themselves

So if Jesus' resurrection is that important, let's look at the evidence for the truth of it. How can we be sure the resurrection of Jesus Christ actually happened and it's not just made up by starry-eyed followers?

Josh McDowell is a Bible scholar of our times who has presented evidence for the resurrection of Christ on college and university campuses and in debates with some of the most convincing skeptics you could find. After more than seven hundred hours of studying this subject to *disprove the resurrection*, he came to the conclusion that the resurrection of Jesus Christ was real. As he states, when it comes to the resurrection of Jesus it is "either one of the most wicked, vicious, heartless hoaxes ever foisted on the minds of human beings—or it is the most remarkable fact of history. You can't have some namby-pamby middle ground. It's either true and mind-blowing, or utterly false and shattering."[1]

---

1 From Josh McDowell, "Evidence for the Resurrection," http://www.leaderu.com/everystudent/easter/articles/josh2.html. Accessed December 2014.

To find out which of these polarized positions is true, we need to ask several more questions and look at the facts.

How Dead Was Jesus?

The first fact we need to look at is deadness. How dead was Jesus? Doubters have questioned whether Jesus really died on the cross. They say that he just fainted or fell into a coma, and the cool air of the tomb revived him. Maybe it was just a near-death experience, and he stopped breathing for a while and then he revived and was fine. Maybe an attending doctor made a mistake, and Jesus wasn't quite dead.

But let's look at who and how many people said that Jesus was as dead as dead could be. First, let's check with the centurion at the crucifixion. He was a commander of a hundred other soldiers and doing the business of crucifixion that day. He saw the sky turn black and felt the earth quake. He saw how Jesus treated people as he hung there and suffered. He watched when Jesus committed his spirit to the Father and breathed his last. This hardened soldier did an about-face, praised God, and declared that Jesus was an innocent man.

After the crucifixion had been going on for many hours, the soldiers under the centurion inspected the bodies, doing the rounds, checking to see if the guilty were dead. If they weren't, the soldiers hurried them along by breaking their legs. They saw that Jesus was already dead (and these men were experts in death); there was no question in their minds. They didn't bother breaking his legs. By the way, that fulfilled a prophecy that not a bone would be broken, although the soldiers likely didn't know much about Hebrew prophecy.

One of the soldiers, just to make sure, ran a spear into Jesus' side. It would have gone up under the rib cage and into Jesus' heart. From the spear hole, blood and fluids poured, underlining the fact that he was dead.

Joseph of Arimathea, a member of the Sanhedrin who had not voted with the group that condemned Jesus, asked Pilate for Jesus' body. Joseph received authorization to remove the body, and he began the embalming process, which was like preparing a mummy. The idea of embalming was to keep air away from the body and delay decay. They wrapped linen strips around and around the body, layer after layer, from head to toe, daubing the strips as they went with embalming ointment, which then hardened. If a person were not dead already, the embalming process would kill him. At the least, it would suffocate a person. Joseph prepared Jesus' body and laid it in a tomb cut into a rock hillside. It was a brand-new, solid-rock tomb, probably one that Joseph had purchased for himself in a preplanned funeral package. There would be no reason to place Jesus' body in a tomb unless Joseph was convinced that the Lord was dead. The spirit had left the body.

A very large stone, probably weighing two tons, was levered into the tomb's opening to close the doorway. The stone was sealed by the Romans. And guards were posted. When we look at the facts of the historical account of the story, any reasonable mind would stipulate that Jesus was dead.

How Empty Was the Tomb?

Dead is one thing, but we've got another fact to contend with. When people went back a few days later, the tomb was empty. The stone was rolled away. The tomb was open. The body was gone.

This stone had three things going for it to keep it mightily in place: (1) it weighed two tons, (2) it was sealed, and (3) it was guarded. That was all done because the Jewish and Roman authorities had heard that Jesus had said he would rise on the third day. With that rumor going around, Pilate and his buddies expected the friends of Jesus to attempt to steal the body so they could claim that Jesus rose from the dead. Then the followers could start a supercult.

The apostle Matthew reported:

> The chief priests and the Pharisees gathered before Pilate and said, "Sir, we remember how that impostor said, while he was still alive, 'After three days I will rise.' Therefore order the tomb to be made secure until the third day, lest his disciples go and steal him away and tell the people, 'He has risen from the dead,' and the last fraud will be worse than the first." Pilate said to them, "You have a guard of soldiers. Go, make it as secure as you can." So they went and made the tomb secure by sealing the stone and setting a guard. (27:62–66)

Of course, if anyone broke the government seal on the tomb, the death penalty was automatic. People didn't play around with this seal. As for the guard, that would be a contingent of sixteen well-trained, disciplined Roman hulks, probably four soldiers at a time, spelling each other off and on around the clock. This was the first-century version of the Navy Seals. These were not guys you'd want to encounter on a dark night.

The guards and the seal were not obstacles that friends of Jesus would take on, even in their boldest hours. And this was definitely not their boldest hour. Jesus' friends were not only not emboldened to take on the guard, they were scattered and in hiding. They had deserted him when he was arrested in the Garden of Gethsemane.

As we saw earlier, Peter, the leader of the gang, had distinguished himself by denying three times during the trials that he even knew who Jesus was. Only John had followed, somewhat shakily, as the procession snaked up Calvary. And finally John crept up close to the cross when Jesus placed the care of his mother into John's hands.

The rest were nowhere to be seen.

This bunch of friends was not about to attempt any heroic deeds. In the days that followed they were hiding behind locked doors, afraid they'd be called before the Jewish and Roman courts and sent to their deaths.

A few women were braver and had followed the burial detail to the tomb, but their intent was to pin down the location so they could bring more spices to anoint the corpse after the Sabbath was over. Their presence was about grieving and paying their last respects to Jesus. Not by any stretch of the imagination could we see these women tackling the guards and shoving aside that stone to make off with the body. Besides lacking strength, they lacked motivation. They weren't interested in a hoax. They had already given up the dream that Jesus was the Messiah, and they were well into the mourning process.

The fact we must face is that on Sunday morning the tomb was empty. The body of Jesus was gone, and the stone was rolled away. Where was he?

But there's another question to ask.

Where Were the Roman Guards?

When the women came at dawn on Sunday morning with their spices, they found that not only was the stone rolled away and the seal broken, but the soldiers were gone. Discipline was second to none in the Roman legions. To desert your duty, to flee your post, even to fall asleep on the job, would provoke the death penalty of the harshest kind. What exactly happened to the soldiers? We don't know, but we do know the story that was concocted for them and we do know about a payoff.

> Some of the guard went into the city and told the chief priests all that had taken place. And when they had assembled with the elders and taken counsel, they gave a sufficient sum of money to the soldiers and said, "Tell people, 'His disciples came by night and stole him away while we were asleep.' And if this comes to the governor's ears, we will satisfy him and keep you out of trouble." So they took the money and did as they were directed. And this story has been spread among the Jews to this day. (Matthew 28:11–15)

Another interesting detail is that when John and Peter finally went to the tomb and looked inside, they found the graveclothes, the linen, and the embalming ointment that Joseph of Arimathea had applied to Jesus' body—all intact. The strips of cloth were lying there and the head wrapping was lying separate. What they saw was like the empty chrysalis of a caterpillar's cocoon, but man-sized.

And There He Is

Then it started. Story after story of Jesus' appearing to people. Mary Magdalene sees him. A few disciples see him. The entire group of disciples sees him, including Thomas, the prince of doubt. Jesus joined a couple of friends on the road to Emmaus. He appeared to more than five hundred people at once. A little later, Paul wrote about this (1 Corinthians 15:6) and noted that most of these people were still alive. He said, "If you don't believe me, ask them."

None of these people expected to see Jesus alive again. These were not weak-headed people given to hallucinations or imaginative fantasies. Even if that description fit one or two, more than five hundred people at the same time don't share the same hallucination. Of course, all of these reports could have been easily refuted if somebody had just produced the body. But apparently nobody had a body to produce. The same line of reasoning holds true in case the women and disciples had made a mistake and gone to the wrong tomb, as some skeptics suggested. To refute that, the authorities merely needed to point to the right tomb with the body inside. They didn't.

Changed Lives

Remember that band of depressed, cowering, frightened, disillusioned, lying, hiding disciples? A short time later we see a completely different group. Peter, the one who said three times, "I don't even know the man," stood courageously on the day of Pentecost and preached to a crowd in Jerusalem, the city where all this went down just fifty days earlier. He minced no words:

> Let all the house of Israel therefore know for certain that God
> has made [Jesus] both Lord and Christ, this Jesus whom you
> crucified. (Acts 2:36)

A bit later he continued this theme: "You killed the Author of life, whom God raised from the dead. To this we are witnesses" (Acts 3:15).

Peter was bold beyond belief. He was accusing people of murder who stood right there in the crowd, people who had the authority to haul him away. Where did this kind of courage come from? It came from being convinced that he had seen the risen Christ and the promised Holy Spirit. And Peter was just one of these changed friends who would go on to deliver the good news of salvation to the ends of the earth and who would suffer for it, but who simply didn't care because it was all so true.

All the disciples, according to sources outside the Bible, suffered martyrdom, except John, who died in exile. People do not die for something they know to be a lie. These men were transformed by the fact that Jesus Christ had risen from the dead.

"That's just it," someone might be saying. "All of the sources sighted above for the resurrection of Jesus are from the writings of his followers in the four gospel accounts—in the Scripture." True. Yet the preponderance of evidence from the changed lives of these followers in real-time history points to a significant, life-altering event. A resurrection.

Your Comeback Linked to His

A woman in our church, Elise, knows firsthand what it means to come back from the brink of death and from the depths of loss. A few years ago she was diagnosed with stage IV pancreatic cancer. It was essentially a death sentence, although oncologists told her she could prolong her life a bit by going through chemotherapy. Elise was absolutely floored. She was vibrant, in early midlife, had a blossoming career, with lots of plans and dreams for the future, especially with her husband and their two young boys.

She asked her doctor how long she might have to live at the most, especially if she submitted to the most aggressive chemo possible. "Most people in your condition don't last more than nine months," he said.

This was her new reality, and it was beyond comprehension. For Elise, death was just not an option she was ready to accept. She knew that a miracle was her only hope.

But God was already at work in her life before Elise realized it. A few days *before* the diagnosis, someone knocked at Elise's door. It was Dwayne, the father of her son's friend, whom she had only spoken to a few times. "You've come to my spirit three times and I know that I need to pray with you," he said.

Elise said okay, and he came in. Her sister-in-law was also there, and just before the man started to pray, she told him, "You may not want to use the whole Jesus thing, because Elise is Jewish."

But Elise said, "That's okay. I'm opening my heart to everything. Pray as you would normally pray."

While the man prayed, Elise, not knowing fully why Dwayne was there, thought to herself, *How incredibly nice to take time out of his day and do this.*

Once diagnosed, desperate for a miracle, Elise and her husband, Patrick, contacted Dwayne and asked him to come over and pray with them. As Dwayne began to pray, Elise began to feel sensation go through her whole body. Elise looked at Dwayne when he finished and asked, "What was that?" Dwayne replied, "God is in your house! God is in your house!" Immediately, both Elise and Patrick felt an overwhelming sense of peace.

After that, Elise started going to church. Although she wasn't ready to accept Jesus yet, she continued opening her heart on her path to faith, learning more about Jesus.

Meanwhile, she did six rounds of aggressive chemo. Elise's scans showed the tumor was shrinking. Elise's sister, Cari, suggested that she get a second opinion from one of the leading pancreatic cancer oncologists—just to make sure she was on the right track. This doctor told her that her doctor was crazy to think that her body could endure another six rounds of chemo. "You won't be able to walk. You won't be able to dress your kids. At the end of the day, you are going to die from this cancer. I suggest that you do a less aggressive chemo treatment and give yourself a better quality of life until you die." Elise was obviously upset but knew that God had a plan.

Elise kept journeying forward and trusting God's plan. She read Jeremiah 29:11 constantly. That following Sunday, I spoke about the story of Lazarus. At the end of the gathering, she was filled with emotion. She told her husband, "I think I got this cancer for God to show a miracle." She felt as though she was just like Lazarus, that she already had one foot in the grave. That day, she accepted Jesus as her Savior.

Months later, Elise took a break from her chemo and radiation treatments to get an accurate scan. It was a difficult month emotionally for her because she felt as though she wasn't fighting. The month became even more difficult when another person she had met who was also battling cancer passed away. Tara was a mother of two kids (ages four and seven). All Elise could think was, *Is that going to be me? Am I going to leave my husband to raise our children by himself?* For three days Elise could not stop crying. On that third evening, Elise cried and prayed all night until she fell asleep.

The next morning, she woke up, looked at her husband, Patrick, and felt an overwhelming sense of peace like she'd never felt before. "I'm okay," she said to him. This burden was completely lifted. The next thing she said was, "I don't think I have cancer anymore." It was an audacious statement, but Elise just knew she was going to be okay.

Two weeks later, Elise went in for scans. But this time was different. For the first time, she didn't feel nervous or anxious. She simply asked God to give her a little bit of good news because she knew that no matter what the results were, she was going to be okay. Her doctor walked in and was clearly blown away by the results. He told her that nothing lit up in her PET scan—she had no active cancer in her body. The cancer was gone.

Completely gone.

That was more than two and a half years ago, and Elise is still cancer free. Jesus is the king of all comebacks, and Elise attributed her comeback directly to Jesus. It was as if her healing was a direct confirmation of her salvation.

Not all of us will experience a miracle of healing like Elise did, but we can all experience a miracle of salvation like she did. Physical healing is sometimes in God's plan for us, but spiritual healing is always in his plan for us. And both are always bound up in Jesus' resurrection.

Jesus' comeback from death, never to die again, ensures that we can come back from the jaws of sin and the death penalty it demands. There is no cancer, no sickness, no sin, no reversal of fortunes, no curse, no heartache—nothing—that's greater than Jesus. Jesus heals. Jesus restores. Jesus brings life.

Scripture promises:

For the creation was subjected to futility, not willingly, but because of him who subjected it, in that the creation itself will be set free from its bondage to corruption and obtain the free-dom of the glory of the children of God. For we know that the whole creation has been groaning together in the pains of childbirth until now. And not only creation, but we our-selves, who have the firstfruits of the Spirit, groan inwardly as we wait eagerly for adoption as sons, the redemption of our bodies. (Romans 8:20–23)

With Jesus, we can come back from, well, actually anything. Here's how we do it:

Just as Christ was raised from the dead by the glory of the Father, we too might walk in newness of life.

For if we have been united with him in a death like his, we shall certainly be united with him in a resurrection like his. (Romans 6:4–5)

Think about it: the ultimate comeback of Jesus Christ from the dead embraces all our personal comebacks. It envelopes them. It simply eats them up. He's alive, and our personal victo-ries are all wrapped up in that. It doesn't matter what you need to come back from or how hopeless it feels.

- When you come back from the bottom of the pit of sin, from the worst ghetto of degradation, from the gutter of gutters, and you move into personal salvation, it's possible because Jesus Christ is alive.
- When you come back from a background of abuse of the worst kind, from victimization that's beyond imagination, into the freedom and beauty of walking with Jesus and

seeing yourself in his image, it's possible because Jesus Christ is alive.

- When you make a comeback from crime, whether you're the victim or the perpetrator, it's because Jesus Christ is alive.

- When you come back from the bottom of the bottle or the depths of the worst stash of drugs ever seen, it's possible because Jesus Christ is alive.

- When you make a comeback from disease and injury and pain, cancer or depression or anorexia, or whatever debilitation you want to name, and come back into blessed normalcy, it's because Jesus Christ is alive.

- When you leave behind the worst personality traits of your heritage and your DNA and make a comeback into a personality that reflects all the fruits of the Spirit—love, joy, peace, patience, kindness, goodness, faithfulness, gentleness, self-control—it's because Jesus Christ is alive.

- When you come back from a relationship breakdown, from the messiest divorce, from estrangement, from deep divisions in your family life, from betrayal, but you survive and move on with a new life, your comeback is because Jesus Christ is alive.

- When you make a comeback from a business failure or a lost job or a lost house or a lost fortune, you move ahead into a new plan for your life with confidence because Jesus Christ is alive.

- When you awaken from a life on autopilot—not terrible in outward appearance, but void of the fullness you know you were created for—and fall in love with Jesus all over again, it's because he is alive.

The ultimate comeback is Jesus Christ, the God-man, walking free from the jaws of death to give us our comebacks. This God always loves us, always cares for us, always offers us mercy and grace. He knows the big picture of everything, and he knows how our lives fit into that big picture. This is the God we're called to love and serve and follow today.

Will you ask him that one question, the same question asked by the thief on the cross, the question you already know the answer to: Jesus, will you remember me today?

That's how your comeback begins.

Will you humble yourself? End your self-devised schemes? Retire from your self-imposed banishment? Admit your zero position? Call out on the one whose comeback makes your comeback a sure thing?

Jesus is alive. Jesus is able. He is here now and your comeback is ready to begin.

ACKNOWLEDGMENTS

At our church, and within our team, we have a culture value that says: we > me. We is greater than me. That's true in all of life, but tangibly visible when a book comes to life. This book is inspired by a series of messages that I shared at Passion City Church. But it's in the form you are holding because my friend, Marcus Brotherton—an accomplished author in his own right—took those talks and notes, combined them with lengthy conversations we shared, and created the framework for what's written on these pages. This partnership not only allowed the book to become a reality, it was a fantastic process, and one for which I am enormously grateful.

As well, I want to say a huge thank-you to everyone who allowed their comeback stories to be shared with the world. They are real people, courageous and inspirational. Their lives beautifully reflect the hope of Jesus and I am honored to help extend their reach and influence through this book.

Shelley and I share this journey, and all the ups and downs that are recounted in these pages. Simply put, she is amazing. Her resilience, brilliance, and grace have paved the way for everything we have been blessed to be part of. She is the love of my life.

Our new Passion Publishing venture is a dream come true and is led by my gifted friend and teammate, Kevin Marks. Kevin has shepherded the process of creating a new publishing venture for Passion and is responsible for jump-starting this book and has kept the project alive.

Our team at Passion City Church, Passion Conferences, and sixstepsrecords is the best. It is a huge privilege to work alongside them day to day. Special thanks to Sue Graddy who helped iron out a lot of the details.

Obviously, a few of the most significant moments in our Passion journey are included in this book. A whole team of people contributed to the success of those events, both staff and Door Holders (volunteers).

And to our new friends at W Publishing Group and HarperCollins Christian Publishing—we are grateful for our partnership. Thank you Mark Schoenwald, David Moberg, and Matt Baugher for believing in this project and helping this message reach people around the world.

Jesus is the reason the word *comeback* is in our vocabulary. He is ultimate in all things, and my hope in these pages is that he will be seen and savored and adored.

I love you, Jesus.

ABOUT THE AUTHOR

A passionate communicator and leader, Louie Giglio is the vision-ary architect and director of the Passion Movement, which includes the collegiate gatherings of Passion Conferences, Atlanta-based Passion City Church, and Capitol CMG label partner sixsteps-records, whose artists include Chris Tomlin, David Crowder, Matt Redman, Kristian Stanfill, Christy Nockels, and Passion.

Through US and international events, Passion conferences invite students around the globe to join with their generation in living for what matters most: the glory of God.

Louie is the author of *The Air I Breathe* and *I Am Not But I Know I Am* and is widely known for the Passion Talk Series DVD messages *Indescribable* and *How Great Is Our God*. As a communicator, Louie speaks for events throughout the United States and around the globe.

A native of Atlanta and a graduate of Georgia State University, Louie has completed postgraduate work at Baylor University and holds a master's degree from Southwestern Baptist Theological Seminary.

Louie and his wife, Shelley, live in Atlanta, Georgia.

EVERYBODY NEEDS A
COMEBACK

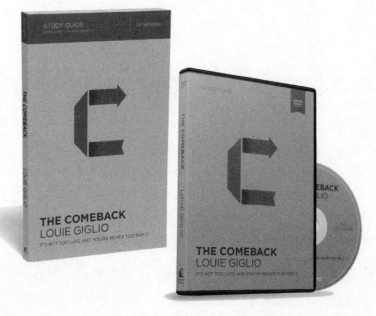

We all know what it feels like when life disappoints us, or to long for something different, something better, something more. In this six-session study, pastor Louie Giglio draws on examples of people from Scripture to show how God is in the business of giving fresh starts. It will offer you encouragement and perspective if you are feeling frustrated or confused, are enduring hardship or pain, have made mistakes or are grieving, or are disappointed and feel you've lost your way.

AVAILABLE IN STORES AND ONLINE!

ALSO AVAILABLE FROM
LOUIE GIGLIO

Join a generation living for
what matters most—the name
and renown of Jesus Christ

passionconferences.com

See all the latest resources from
Passion Conferences, Passion City Church,
and sixstepsrecords.

passionresources.com